D0289596

Contemporary Studies in Literature

Eugene Ehrlich, *Columbia University*
Daniel Murphy, *City University of New York*
Series Editors

Volumes include:

T. S. Eliot

a collection of criticism edited by Linda W. Wagner

McGraw-Hill Book Company

New York • St. Louis • San Francisco • London • Düsseldorf

Kuala Lumpur • Mexico • Montreal • Panama • São Paulo

Sydney • Toronto • Johannesburg • New Delhi • Singapore

123456789MUMU7987654

Library of Congress Cataloging in Publication Data

Wagner, Linda Welshimer, comp.

  T. S. Eliot: a collection of criticism

  (Contemporary studies in Literature)
  CONTENTS: Mizener, A. To meet Mr. Eliot.–Bergonzi,
B. T. S. Eliot: the early poems.–Rosenthal, M. L.
"The waste land" as an open structure. [etc.]

  1. Eliot, Thomas Stearns, 1888-1965–Criticism and
interpretation.
PS3509.L43Z889   821'.9'12   74-724
ISBN 0-07-067675-5

Preface

Choosing essays on T. S. Eliot's work in 1974 is even more difficult than the task would have been several years before. Recent events have generated new interest in this poet. In 1971, the previously lost work sheets for *The Waste Land* were published by Valerie Eliot, the poet's widow, and many readers were fascinated with tracing the changes that had occurred through the versions of this important poem. This publication was followed quickly by the fifty-year commemorative issues of several journals of criticism. (*The Waste Land* was originally published in 1922.) Critics who had not written about Eliot for many years were called on for judgments, and many were eager to make general observations about Eliot's influence on modern poetics as well as to assess the impact of the early poem.

Of the nine essays in this collection, six have been published since 1969. Of the others, Mizener's "To Meet Mr. Eliot" is one of the best introductions to the poet ever written, and Leonard Unger's article is the contribution of a critic whose work on Eliot has always been admired for its sanity. Pound's note on the 1917 *Prufrock and Other Poems* is a fine example of the criticism of the times in which Pound wrote, when pointing out directions and influences (and discussing one's own poetics) was more important than any explication of text.

The very recent essays, too, are generally more than explication. (Criticism of Eliot's work has finally reached that higher plateau where the critic can assume that his reader shares a basic understanding of the poem in question.) M. L. Rosenthal places *The Waste Land* in a new perspective, seeing it as an "open," suggestive poem (one in which knowing all the literal references may still not re-create the poetic experience for a reader); Daniel Schwarz questions the accepted reading of "Gerontion"; Katharine Worth discusses the actual dramatic values of Eliot's plays; and William T. Moynihan both explicates and marks directions for much of *Four Quartets*. I think the length of this latter essay is justified. Even though *Four Quartets* has come to be considered

Eliot's most important poem, readers frequently are less familiar with this work than with earlier collections of Eliot's poetry. It also was a personal pleasure to be able to include the essays by Dame Helen Gardner and Bernard Bergonzi. I regret being unable to excerpt a selection from one of the best recent books on Eliot, Gertrude Patterson's *T. S. Eliot: Poems in the Making* (1971).

Many of the essays collected here, written during the last few years, benefit from the most recent scholarship on Eliot. Since there is to be no authorized biography of the writer, the next important contribution will be publication of Eliot's letters, of which there are thousands. Until Valerie Eliot completes the project of collecting these, scholars will have to rely on present judgments. Some extremely useful bibliographies on Eliot have been published during the last few years. Donald Gallup's new edition of the Eliot bibliography remains a classic study, and there are many bibliographies describing the recent work on Eliot in languages other than English (see, for example, Richard Ludwig's "T. S. Eliot" in *Sixteen Modern American Authors*). Published in 1972 was Mildred Martin's *A Half-Century of Eliot Criticism, 1916-1965.* Because the hundreds of books and essays included there are helpfully annotated, I have limited the bibliography of my own collection to only the most recent books on Eliot, many of them not included in Martin's study.

I do regret that the entire subject of Eliot's essays, both literary and social, has had to be ignored in this present collection. Three recent books give valuable aid to the reader who is interested in the prose side of the poet: John D. Margolis' *T. S. Eliot's Intellectual Development, 1922-1939* (1972); Allen Austin's *T. S. Eliot, The Literary and Social Criticism* (1971); and Bernard Bergonzi's *T. S. Eliot* (1972). It seems increasingly evident that no clear picture of the poet can be drawn unless one considers the great amount of writing he was doing in addition to the major poems and plays.

L. W. W.

Michigan State University
January, 1974

Contents

T.S. Eliot

Linda Wagner

Introduction

Thomas Stearns Eliot is a member of a select group. He is an author with much more written about his work than he has himself written. This ratio places him in the company of Shakespeare, Chaucer, Milton, Dante, Balzac, Dostoevski, James Joyce, and other masters of literature. Eliot could have filled one bookshelf with his own books; then he would have needed an entire wall to house the various commentaries on those books. And if the past thirty years have produced so many critical studies, what can we expect in the next 130 years?

What prompts so much comment? Why are scholars the world over intrigued with Eliot's comparatively few poems, his five plays, and his essays? It is not, surely, only the fact that the poems were "modern" that has attracted readers. Innovative as Eliot was in many of his poems, he was doing the same kinds of things Ezra Pound, Wallace Stevens, Carl Sandburg, William Carlos Williams, and countless other writers were doing. Neither is his readership based on the fact that Eliot himself was a legendary figure who created interest in his writing because of his own life. On the contrary, Eliot was hardly romantic. He worked first in a bank and later as editor for a publishing house; he spent much of his life and energy concerned about his wife's increasingly poor health. (And his own health was never good because of congenital hernia and tachycardia—rapid heart.)

No, Eliot's writing has attracted so many readers not because of his innovation or his charisma but rather because in each major poem he managed to capture the mood, the sentiment, of an age. People can read his poems and respond to them—"Yes, that's it exactly"—even though the poems are comparatively "difficult." They do contain references a reader needs help to understand; they often range widely from present experiences to historical ones; structurally, they often are juxtaposed images instead of a continuing narrative. But readers manage to work their ways into and through these poems because Eliot wrote

1

about timeless ideas and themes: living a meaningful life; finding a personal religion; understanding love and death. In so doing, he created memorable characters and equally memorable passages of poetry.

One of the main criticisms of the poetry that started being published sixty years ago was that free verse supposedly was a gimmick. The public suspected that these poems were made haphazardly, without thought; and they questioned whether or not these "modern" poets indeed had anything to say. With most of Eliot's poems, a fairly weighty and recognizable idea presents itself somewhere in the poem, chiefly because Eliot tended to write longer poems than other modern poets did. The poet can make more of an impression on even an unfriendly reader in three pages than he can in eight or nine lines. Seeing the radical changes that were occurring in the form of poetry, some readers may have championed Eliot as the best of a bad lot. Other readers, those excited by the use of blank or free verse, recognized Eliot's genuine ability, especially in his control of the whole poem. For still others, Eliot was someone to read because Ezra Pound, a more established poet and critic, was pushing his work. For the British reader, Eliot was not only a poet; he was also a tactful, socially adept, and gentlemanly person. (Some young writers of the period had already offended many established literary figures.) But the primary reason Eliot made such an impression on the literary world (and not only on the English-speaking world) was the 1922 publication of *The Waste Land.*

I will try here briefly to describe 1922. Joyce's novel *Ulysses,* after several years of pornography charges, was also published in 1922, and it is difficult to tell which caused the greater furor, *Ulysses* or *The Waste Land.* What Eliot had caught, in his nineteen-page poem, was the deflated mood of an American people that had moved from optimism to cynicism in the four years following the end of World War I, "the war to end all wars." "Uncle Sam" had stepped in to save the world; Woodrow Wilson had engineered the relatively ineffective Fourteen Points and the resulting peace. By 1922, people knew the peace was less than promising. The world was filled with rhetoric; young Americans were living abroad, protesting both prohibition and the materialism of postwar prosperity. Those who did stay in America were (supposedly) drinking illegally in speakeasies, taking unchaperoned jaunts in automobiles, wearing outrageous clothes, and, above all, abandoning any belief in God. This was the generation hardest hit by Darwin's 1859 *Origin of Species* (witness the bitter Scopes trial in 1925), and some of the dissension among parents and children in the twenties grew from the shakiness of formal religious beliefs.

The Waste Land presented a dark, despairing picture of what was viewed as the American culture. (There are many references in the poem to English and Continental locations, however.) It included scenes of loveless sex, lonely people, sinister predictions, and death; and its dominant image was the barren and sterile land, waiting for rain (a symbol of both religious and sexual fulfillment). Even though Eliot managed to shade the poem to a fairly affirmative conclusion, readers found little joy in the "Give. Sympathize. Control." of the closing. They chose, many of them, to read *The Waste Land* as a despairing poem.

So great was the impact of *The Waste Land* that, from 1922 on, whatever Eliot wrote was news. Yet he was then writing little poetry because of his editorship of *The Criterion* and, perhaps more importantly, because of his further struggles in what one critic has called his "long process of self-definition." "The Hollow Men," built from fragments of *The Waste Land,* is admittedly one of Eliot's bleakest poems. It closes with the lines, *This is the way the world ends/Not with a bang but a whimper.*

In 1927, Eliot found some resolutions to his personal quandaries. He became a British subject and was baptized and confirmed in the Church of England. The difficult affirmation of *Ash-Wednesday,* written from 1927 to 1930, illustrates his new acceptance of his faith and of himself.

For the next few years, Eliot's energies went into *The Criterion,* his beginning work as dramatist (*The Rock* and *Murder in the Cathedral*), and a developing social consciousness. Then, in 1936, came "Burnt Norton," the first of his *Four Quartets.* Once again, with the publication in book form of this, his last major poem (published in 1943 in the United States and in 1944 in England), Eliot perfectly caught the desperate mood of the times. For England in 1944, World War II was a continuing horror: wasted cities, terrific casualties, and incredible civilian suffering. Coming at the end of four years of continuous anxiety, Eliot's quiet profession of personal faith answered an almost universal need. Like a dignified and reassuring tone poem, these four poems probe eternal questions and answer them through the best of Christian philosophy. The poetry is, once again, innovative. Eliot was attempting fresh techniques and devices. In *Four Quartets* a more leisurely rhythm dominates. The use of the concrete image is now subordinated to the reflecting voice, moving discursively, remembering, cajoling, pausing to make a point:

> At the still point of the turning world. Neither flesh nor
>   fleshless;
> Neither from nor towards; at the still point, there the dance
>   is . . .

Eliot had found his peace, the peace that had been his aim when as a young man he wrote that he wanted to find a good psychiatrist, someone to help him

> use all my energy without waste, to be *calm* when there is nothing
> to be gained by worry, and to concentrate without effort . . . .[1]

One of the many paradoxes—ironies—of Eliot's life and career was that he had these admittedly great personal problems even while he was writing such quietly jubilant poems of faith. As a promising young scholar, instead of finishing the Ph.D., he became a poet, lived abroad, married an Englishwoman—in short, he convinced his parents that he had made "a mess" of his life (and the terms of his father's will clearly showed that parental displeasure).[2]

The marriage on which he had seemingly staked his happiness was hardly idyllic. Vivien, his wife, was often ill and finally was institutionalized. There were no children. Eliot separated from Vivien in 1932, but he did not remarry until 1957. His second, extremely happy marriage to Valerie Eliot took place when he was 69, after Vivien had been dead for nearly ten years.

For most of Eliot's early adult life, he had severe worries about money. During the day, he worked in the foreign services department of a bank; in the evening, he taught the equivalent of our night classes and wrote a great deal of literary journalism—all the while concerned about Vivien's health, his parents' opinions, and his neglect of his major writing, the poetry. It came as no surprise to people who knew Eliot in the twenties that *The Waste Land* was written primarily as a personal poem and only incidentally as social commentary. As Eliot himself said of the poem:

[1] From T. S. Eliot's letter to his brother Henry, 13 December 1921, quoted in *T. S. Eliot, The Waste Land, A Facsimile and Transcript,* ed. Valerie Eliot (New York: Harcourt Brace Jovanovich, 1971), p. xxii.
[2] Eliot to John Quinn, 6 January 1919, quoted in *ibid.,* p. xvi.

> Various critics have done me the honour to interpret the poem in terms of criticism of the contemporary world, have considered it, indeed, as an important bit of social criticism. To me it was only the relief of a personal and wholly insignificant grouse against life; it is just a piece of rhythmical grumbling.[3]

An important insight into the supposed obscurity of Eliot's poetry might be gained here. According to the poet, *The Waste Land* expressed his own disillusion, his own physical *angst*. Yet, unlike more recent poets such as Robert Lowell and Sylvia Plath (poets termed *confessional* by critics), Eliot did not identify his own experiences. He did not obviously use himself as the persona of the poem. Instead, he turned to experiences and characters drawn from past literature and history to tell parts of his story for him. His use of allusion and historical reference seems to have been less a pretentious device than it was a necessary shifting of attention away from his own personal life.

Few readers saw Eliot as a man living an incipient tragedy. He was often pictured as cold and unapproachable—dryly businesslike, with no sense of humor. Friends deny that image and tell many stories of his wit and his love of a good joke. Many young writers benefited from his willingness to help them when he could and his continuing interest in new currents of art.

Perhaps strangely, many people disliked Eliot for having said that he was a "royalist" in politics and an "Anglo-Catholic" in religion. They used this conservatism to negate the wide-ranging curiosity of Eliot's mind. Eliot had made his final choice of belief not out of intellectual laziness but rather with intimate knowledge of a number of philosophies, both Eastern and Western. Granted the fact that most writers pride themselves on liberalism, such a stance should not mandate specific political or religious alliances. Above all, the literate man must respect freedom of choice.

As poet, too, Eliot experienced many ironies in his career. Trained as a philosopher at Harvard, he might never have been a poet at all. His dissertation (on the philosophy of F. H. Bradley) had been approved, and he had only to return from England to take his oral examination; but his ship was canceled because of World War I sea peril, and he never returned to receive the degree.

Eliot's beginning as poet was also slow. His earliest poems could not find a publisher, even though Conrad Aiken, a Harvard classmate and poet, had sponsored them. Finally, in 1914, Eliot met Ezra Pound, who

[3]Ibid., p. 1.

sent several of his poems to *Poetry* and ordered that they be published (Pound was Foreign Editor of the magazine). The editor there did not like the poems, among them "The Love Song of J. Alfred Prufrock," but she respected Pound's judgment, and so, after several delays, the poems were published.

Eliot's first collection, *Prufrock and Other Poems* (1917), was not a popular book by any means. Few copies were sold. Yet the title poem probably has been included in more anthologies than has any other modern poem in any language. In fact, each of Eliot's major poems— "Prufrock," *The Waste Land, Ash-Wednesday,* and *Four Quartets*—received, on first publication, as much negative comment as praise. Few writers have so divided the critical world. (One collection of essays on *The Waste Land* is entitled, *Storm over The Waste Land.*) But, somewhat surprisingly, after ten or fifteen years, the praise in each case buried the faultfinding; and now Eliot's reputation rides higher than ever. He is the only American poet ever to have been awarded the Nobel Prize for Literature (1948).

Yet even that statement is tinged with irony, for Eliot is often considered a British writer rather than an American one. Granted, he became a British subject in 1927, when he was 39; but he often wrote with kindness of his early years and of his native country. Descended from the illustrious William Greenleaf Eliot, founder of both Washington University and the first Unitarian church in St. Louis, Eliot was highly conscious of the position his family had maintained both in St. Louis and, earlier, in Boston. Like his ancestors, Eliot was interested in education, religion, and politics. He was vehement about the dangers of fascism and communism, even during the 1930s, when many writers looked with favor on these ideologies.

As editor of *The Criterion* from 1922 to 1939, Eliot often used its columns for broad social commentary; he was seldom guilty of ivory tower attitudes. Indeed, one of the primary reasons Eliot wrote relatively few poems was that his interests after the 1920s swung increasingly away from literature and toward theology, education, politics, economics, and foreign affairs. First in his many essays and then in drama, Eliot found ways of reaching wider audiences and less elite readers than his poems had attracted. He also found a method, particularly in *Murder in the Cathedral* and *The Rock,* of expressing his religious commitment. As early as 1930, Eliot had said firmly,

> the "truest" philosophy is the best material for the greatest poet; . . . the poet must be rated in the end both by the philosophy

> he realizes in poetry and by the fullness and adequacy of the realization.[4]

The greatest poet's work would never be a mere showcase for new techniques; it would speak with the Christianity which was for Eliot the " 'truest' philosophy." And, ideally, it would speak to an audience trained ethically as well as intellectually:

> Unless popular education is also moral education, it is merely putting firearms into the hands of children. For education in History is in vain, unless it teaches us to extract . . . moral and spiritual values from History.[5]

That Eliot was capable of expressing these ideas in some of the best poetry of our age may be reason enough to explain his wide and continuing appeal.

[4] T. S. Eliot, "Poetry and Propaganda," *Bookman*, 70 (February, 1930), 595-602.

[5] T. S. Eliot, "Commentary," *Criterion*, 10 (1931), 309.

Arthur Mizener

To Meet Mr. Eliot

Nearly forty years ago, setting out to make a case for Ben Jonson,
Mr. Eliot observed that "the reputation of Jonson has been of the most
deadly kind that can be compelled upon the memory of a poet," and
went on to describe that reputation as "the most perfect conspiracy of
approval." For anyone who grew up with Mr. Eliot's poetry, responding
to it profoundly and looking on its author almost with awe, it comes as
a shock to find that a similar conspiracy against Mr. Eliot is beginning
to be organized. Yet I think it has to be admitted that for many readers
Mr. Eliot is beginning to seem an elder statesman of letters, a Great Man
to whom the newspapers—as they did last spring—refer as a "68-year-
old poet and playwright," almost as if he were another Poet among
School Children, looked upon with uncomprehending respect as a man
no longer expected to contribute anything the spectators care enough
about to quarrel with.

This attitude is likely to seem an outrageous indignity to those of us
for whom Mr. Eliot's poetry has always been an immediately moving
experience. But we know from what happened, for example, to Tennyson's reputation that to meet history's conspiracy of approval with
indignation will not do; it only makes matters worse. If we are to
preserve the greatness of Mr. Eliot's poetry for readers who have not
known the experience from which that greatness emerges, we are going
to have to recognize that some of the elements in his poetry which
seemed to appeal directly to our most private sentiments now sometimes persuade people that it is too much the poetry of a period's

Reprinted by permission from The Sewanee Review, *65 (Winter, 1957),
34-49. Copyright* ©*1957 by the University of the South.*

sentiment. For thirty years we have taken it pretty much for granted that every reader found himself in immediate touch with the moving center of Mr. Eliot's poetry and have devoted ourselves to sharpening the reader's awareness of what moved him. What is now beginning to be needed is an approach to Mr. Eliot's poetry which will be of use to readers who are separated from it by what he once called "the burden of respectability" its very success has imposed on it. When one can read "with pleasure and edification" even an address to Mr. Wilkinson's spade by Mr. Eliot, it is difficult to adopt the attitude this purpose requires; it asks of us some of the detachment Mr. Eliot himself has always cultivated, not least successfully in the comments on his own work in his most recent essay, "The Frontiers of Criticism."[1]

This acute "historical" sense of his own work goes back a long way with Mr. Eliot. As early as 1931 he was saying, "when I wrote a poem called *The Waste Land*, some of the more approving critics said I had expressed the 'disillusionment of a generation,' which is nonsense. I may have expressed for them their illusion of being disillusioned, but that did not form part of my intention." It is understandable that so serious a poet as Mr. Eliot was distressed to find himself confused with people like Aldous Huxley (whom he described at that time as "a depressing life-forcer") and thought of as disillusioned in the way popular writers of the twenties were. Mr. Eliot's poetry did not, certainly, express this popular disillusionment, but it did speak to something in its age more potent than either that age's opinions—most of which Mr. Eliot disliked—or its sentimentalities; it achieved its greatness by penetrating to the very heart of its own times. If longing and terror, glory and horror, are permanent, they none the less exist for each age in its own dialect; Mr. Eliot's lifelong effort to preserve the dialect of the tribe has not been conducted in a foreign language.

The most striking characteristic of his verse has always been its relevance, and this relevance has been achieved by the constant submission of his fine perception to the discipline of his intelligence. His early criticism is deeply concerned with the nature of this kind of discipline and is insistent on the need for an unremitting cultivation of what he once called "the two forms of self-consciousness ["which must go together"], knowing what we are and what we ought to be." It is difficult not to believe that Mr. Eliot's main means for cultivating this self-consciousness—despite his expressed preference for a single regional culture—has been the deliberate movement from one urban culture to another.

[1] In *The Sewanee Review* (Autumn, 1956).

But this is a guess. We know something of Mr. Eliot's history (there is a biographical note in F. O. Mathiessen's book), but very little of the kind of man he has been: the revealing indulgences of vanity in his career have been few and obscure and his friends have been remarkably discreet. There are a few glimpses of him as a young man, for instance, in Conrad Aiken's recollection of him as

> a singularly attractive, tall, and rather dapper young man; with a somewhat Lamian smile, who reeled out of the doorway of the Lampoon on a spring evening, and, catching sight of me, threw his arms about me.... "And that," observed my astonished companion, "if Tom remembers it tomorrow, will cause him to suffer agonies of shyness." And no doubt it did: for he *was* shy.

A couple of years later, we hear, he was going to Boston debutante parties as a discipline for this shyness, and for the same reason learning to box and—in his own phrase—"to swarm with passion up a rope." In another year or two he is writing Conrad Aiken from Oxford: "Come, let us desert our wives, and fly to a land where there are no Medici prints, nothing but concubinage and conversation. Oxford is very pretty, but I don't like to be dead." Not long after, we catch a few more glimpses of him as a young poet around London, smiling what Wyndham Lewis called his "Giaconda smile" in Pound's small, triangular sitting room, content, apparently, to listen while Pound talked.

There are certain things which stand out in these glimpses of what Mr. Eliot was like before he completed his public persona. There is the sensibility, so energetic that it constantly overflows into an extravagance for which he feels apologetic. There is the vigorous, disciplinary self-consciousness with which he strives to control both his extravagance and his temperamental shyness. And there is the repeated shift from one urban culture to another, from Harvard to the Sorbonne, from Marburg to Oxford, and the effort to make the sensibility grow up to and into it—"mixing memory and desire."

Mr. Eliot began his life in an environment which must have had some of the heightened consciousness of its cultural inheritance characteristic of exiled groups. As he himself pointed out in his introduction to his mother's poem, *Savonarola*, Charlotte Stearns brought with her from Boston its nineteenth-century compound of "Schleiermacher, Emerson, Channing, and Herbert Spencer." The Eliots' awareness of this tradition must have been intensified by the very different air of St. Louis, just as their awareness of that air must have been intensified by their Boston inheritance. Thus for Mr. Eliot, even "the penny world

I bought/To eat with Pipit behind the screen" was not a simple one to be accepted without critical self-consciousness. The Harvard and Boston of his undergraduate years must have offered him a yet more complex conception of his tradition's memory to adapt desire to and a more imposing sense of the recalcitrance of the everyday world and our everyday selves. The process of adaptation and complication of which we can catch glimpses here was to be deliberately repeated again and again in his life.

As a consequence his poems have always been constructed around the contrasts among different ways of life which he has possessed as experience. The young man who submitted himself to the discipline of Boston parties knew the world of "Cousin Nancy" Ellicott, who "smoked/And danced all the modern dances"; he also knew the world of "Matthew and Waldo, guardians of the faith,/The army of unalterable law" which Cousin Nancy altered without even knowing it—*by* not knowing it. Whatever Charlotte Stearns' son may think of Nancy, she is his cousin and he knows from both propinquity and deliberately acquired experience the power she possesses. Most of Eliot's early poems know better the power of the Bleisteins than the ineffectuality of the Burbanks, are more acutely aware of "what we are" than hopeful of our ability to realize "what we ought to be." What can the poor old aunts, who "were not quite sure how they felt about it," do about Nancy's crude energy which leaves Matthew and Waldo on the shelf, unhonored sybils hanging in their basket, and leaves nowhere Meredith's assurance that the stars in their courses assert eternal providence? Let Prufrock walk among the lowest of the dead and Burbank meditate on his decayed house; Sweeney and Bleistein are up and doing, men not easily to be persuaded to consider the seven laws of architecture or the word others have found swaddled within the darkness of the world.

Thus, in a way fundamentally characteristic of American experience, the abyss between the idea and the reality of Mr. Eliot's world increased; as his sensibility was subdued to an increasingly complex conception of Western Culture, the world of his everyday experience appeared more monstrous and remote. No wonder he came to feel that "we live in an incredible public world and an intolerable private world." However reluctant a man may be to move toward such despair, this course appears to be nearly unavoidable for the gifted provincial writer who seeks to acquire the memory of his whole culture and to discipline desire to it. This feeling is as evident in such different poets as Hart Crane and Allen Tate as it is in Mr. Eliot. That Mr. Eliot faced it honestly and without sentimentality is a great triumph of intelligence and integrity; that he found an unaffected and effective way out of it is perhaps even a greater triumph.

At its responsible best, the repeated adaptation of the feelings to a more complicated conception of tradition produces a sensibility different from that of either the original or the adopted culture. Mr. Eliot's perceptions characteristically have the precision and self-consciousness of a foreigner speaking a language nearly perfectly:

> Now the light falls
> Across the open field, leaving the deep lane
> Shuttered with branches, dark in the afternoon. . . .
> In a warm haze, the sultry light
> Is absorbed, not refracted, by grey stone.   ("East Coker," I)

This is a man for whom what he sees has, for all its familiarity, some element of the alien about it, so that he notices still, almost with surprise, that the light "is absorbed, not refracted, by grey stone." Mr. Eliot's possession of his tradition has this same air. It has been acquired, as fully acquired as a fine intelligence and a powerful will can make it. But it is acquired, and it never becomes entirely habitual. As a result, Mr. Eliot's perceptions have a very special kind of brilliance.

Step by step, "by a continual surrender of himself as he [was] at the moment to something which [was] more valuable," Mr. Eliot committed himself to the fullest conception of Western Culture he could grasp. As he presently realized, with a care for emotional honesty that perhaps only the heir of American Unitarianism would have, this included Catholic Christianity. "Culture," as Mr. Eliot said, "after all, is not enough, even though nothing is enough without culture."

From the beginning of his career, Mr. Eliot's prose has given us a commentary of remarkable vividness on this process of adaptation. As he himself observed in "The Frontiers of Criticism," "the best of my *literary* criticism . . . consists of essays on poets and poetic dramatists who had influenced me." The epigraph of the first essay in his first book of criticism—"Eriger en lois ses impressions personnelles, c'est le grand effort d'un homme s'il est sincère"—sums up his whole policy as a poet. In one of his earliest essays, "Tradition and the Individual Talent," he made the purpose behind that policy quite clear. "Poetry," he said, "is not a turning loose of emotion, but an escape from emotion; it is not the expression of a personality, but an escape from personality." "But, of course," he added, "only those who have personality and emotions know what it means to want to escape these things."

Some odd combination of slyness and humility frequently leads Mr.
Eliot to treat the crucial point of his argument this way, as if it were
self-evident and could almost be thrown away. But the point here is
clear enough. The way to avoid being "laid waste by the anarchy of
feeling" is, in life, the discipline of an adequate culture. In verse, the
escape from this disorder is an adequate form, a form which provides
impersonal occasions and motives unrelated to the writer's for what he
wants to express. This is not a theory for writing poetry without
involving the personality and the emotions (as the term "escape" might
conceivably suggest); it is a theory for writing a poetry which makes the
best use of them by giving them the greatest formal and therefore
public order.

The ordering form of Mr. Eliot's verse derives immediately from
Ezra Pound's imagism. Pound's imagism is only one manifestation of an
almost mystical theory of perception which is one of the remarkable
phenomena of our time. From James's "represent" through Joyce's
"epiphanies" and Mr. Eliot's "objective correlative" to Hemingway's
"the way it was," our writers have been dominated by a belief that
every pattern of feeling has its pattern of objects and events, so that if
the writer can set down the pattern of objects in exactly the right
relations, without irrelevances or distortions, they will evoke in the
reader the pattern of feelings. Whatever the limitations of this view—
and we have hardly considered seriously yet what they may be—it
suited Mr. Eliot's talent, with its great powers of visual and aural
perception.

The early poems, in *Prufrock* and *Poems,* are either short lyrics or
dramatic monologues. As we read through the lyrics, we see Mr. Eliot
moving from the relatively simple contrasts of Cousin Nancy with
Arnold and Emerson to something more complicated. In "Sweeney
Erect," for example, we seen Sweeney indifferently shaving while the
woman in his bed has an epileptic fit. The poem's judgment of
Sweeney's mode of life is implicit in Mr. Eliot's image of it. But he
reinforces this image, first with a reference to Emerson's "Self-Reli-
ance," and then with an extravagant figure, a comparison of Sweeney
and Theseus:

> Display me Aeolus above
>   Reviewing the insurgent gales
> Which tangle Ariadne's hair
>   And swell with haste the perjured sails.

The full realized sorrow of romantic betrayal which is embodied in the Ariadne story gives us a further measure of the mean vanity of the ladies and Mrs. Turner, of Doris's inadequate goodheartedness, and of Sweeney's complacent and innocent confidence that he "knows the female temperament."

But the Ariadne story is not reality for us, or not the necessary whole of it, any more than is the language in which it is presented here. We notice the delicate emphasis on the original meanings of "reviewing" and "insurgent," the excessively verbal wit of the transferred epithet in the last line, the conventional tragic irony of the contrast between the wind's blowing Ariadne's lovely hair and Theseus' impatient ship. This is a pastiche of Jacobean verse, too skillful to be taken only as parody and too evidently artificial to be taken as wholly straightforward. Its point is reinforced by the poem's epigraph from *The Maid's Tragedy*. Mr. Eliot has always reluctantly admired Beaumont and Fletcher's skill and disapproved of what he considers their lack of integrity ("the blossoms of Beaumont and Fletcher's imagination . . . are cut and slightly withered flowers stuck into sand"). In *The Maid's Tragedy* the deserted heroine comes upon her waiting women at work on a tapestry of Ariadne's story. She assures them their Ariadne is not nearly pathetic enough, makes an eloquent speech offering herself as a model ("and behind me,/Make all a desolation. See, see, wenches," as the first quarto has it), and strikes a theatrically pathetic pose. Mr. Eliot's conviction that this scene is, for all its effectiveness, false is clear from the way he quotes the folio reading of Aspatia's remark out of context: "And behind me/Make all a desolation. Look, look, wenches!"

The world of Sweeney and his woman is brutally limited, almost apish, for all its humanity and "naturalness," but the dream of a world in which Theseus and Ariadne conduct themselves with tragic splendor has a way of turning artificially pretty. If there is in the Ariadne story at its best a suggestion of human possibilities which make Sweeney's world look brutish, there is in Sweeney's story an honesty about the primitive foundation of man's nature which makes very clear the affectations of the Ariadne story at its worst.

What Mr. Eliot does with the dramatic monologue can be illustrated with "Gerontion." "Gerontion" is an immensely skillful "impersonalizing" adaptation of the Jacobean dramatic soliloquy. The weary old man who speaks it is a character remote from Mr. Eliot himself, and both this character, with his long memory and his imprisoning Pyrrhonism, and the form, with its convention of free association, are remarkably suited to the impersonal expression of Mr. Eliot's *impressions per-sonnelles,* his sense of what has gone wrong with the human situation in his own time and must therefore have been what menaced it with greater or less success in other times. "Gerontion" is a powerful and moving expression of these emotions, and it gains a good deal, at least in a negative way, by not presenting them to us merely as the poet's opinions. It shows an astonishing awareness of the images of our world which evoke most powerfully its special kind of despair, and Mr. Eliot mixes these images with just the kind of endless speculation to which Gerontion's state of mind drives us—"These matters that with myself I too much discuss/Too much explain." The brilliance with which the poem exemplifies such speculations is evident if we compare the most famous of them, the passage which begins "After such knowledge, what forgiveness?" with the less effective expression of this thought the different requirements of *The Rock* led Mr. Eliot to write:

> All our knowledge brings us nearer to our ignorance,
> All our ignorance brings us nearer to death,
> But nearness to death no nearer to GOD.
> Where is the Life we have lost in living?
> Where is the wisdom we have lost in knowledge?
> Where is the knowledge we have lost in information?

"Gerontion" is a triumph of transforming a set of personal convictions into an expression which is valid for anyone in our time and perhaps valid for men in all times who have seen what always exists, the solid evidence that the human situation is not a very easy one.

But one does not have to share Professor Winters' feeling about pseudo-reference to feel that a dramatic monologue, deprived as it is of the defining context a soliloquy has, must create within its own limits a sharp impression of the speaker's character if the poet is to have all the benefits of his dramatic disguise. "Gerontion" does not do so. From the first lines, the poem carries such a burden of symbolic meaning that it is difficult to read as the speech of a realized character. Mr. Edmund Wilson has been taken to task for not recognizing that Mr. Eliot's poems are dramatic monologues and complaining that Mr. Eliot talked like an old man at forty. But the fact is that "Gerontion" is in large part only nominally dramatic, almost as if there were some deficiency in Mr. Eliot's sense of the ordinary, immediate reality of people, as if he saw them always as grotesques answering to names like Mrs. Phlaccus and Professor Channing-Cheetah. "The dramatist," he once said quite rightly, "need not understand people; but he must be exceptionally aware of them." Mr. Eliot, to use his own words, is often exceptionally aware only of "the reality of the moral synthesis . . . behind the motions of his personages."

In both subject and form *The Waste Land* is "Gerontion" writ large. It is Mr. Eliot's fullest and most eloquent presentation of the contrasting worlds of Burbank and Bleistein and of the despair the contemplation of that contrast induces; and it is a dramatic monologue with a speaker who is, as Mr. Eliot's note says, "not indeed a 'character' " who must nonetheless unite all the rest. But in *The Waste Land* Mr. Eliot is beginning to elaborate the seasonal image which appears sporadically in "Gerontion" and to substitute for the character of the speaker, which provides the structure for the conventional dramatic monologue, a pattern of reiterated images. This form is given its fullest development in the *Four Quartets* where it shows to greatest advantage.

With *The Waste Land* and "The Hollow Men" Mr. Eliot's career reached a crisis. The Tiresias who helplessly foresuffers all is the final term in a series which begins with Prufrock. Whether Bleistein and Sweeney know it or not, there is no further to go in this desert. But it was five years before Mr. Eliot began, in *Ash-Wednesday,* to find where else to go. If the speaker in *Ash-Wednesday* cannot yet discipline "the lost heart" that "stiffens and rejoices/In the lost lilac and the lost sea voices," even when he does not "wish to wish these things," he is not sure he knows what the right wish is ("Teach us to care and not to care/Teach us to sit still") and is freshly aware of that "Jansenism of the individual biography," as Mr. Eliot calls it in his essay on the *Pensées,* which may have led him to this echo of Pascal. Though *Ash-Wednesday* is also a dramatic monologue, its effects depend very little on the independent character of the speaker; insofar as they do, the coherence of the speaker's voice and manner are enough to support them.

Considering how deeply Mr. Eliot must have been personally involved in the emotions *Ash-Wednesday* is made of, its scrupulous honesty—after all the fundamental purpose for Mr. Eliot's "impersonality"—is a remarkable achievement. These bones sing as truly as they can, but their singing is "chirping/With the burden of the grasshopper" in the waste land, where desire shall fail because memory has. No more than the prophet can the poem say whether these bones shall live; but they can sit still, "forgetting themselves and each other, united/In the quiet of the desert."

It was nearly a decade before Mr. Eliot brought his whole personality and all his feelings under the control of this conception. This was the most formidable disciplining of the sensibility he had attempted, and its cost must have been an effort of the imagination difficult to conceive. Its reward was the *Four Quartets*. Formally, too, the *Four Quartets*—despite the title's refusal to claim more than a loose coherence for them—is remarkable, both because the unobtrusive speaker of the poem has the whole of Mr. Eliot's public reputation behind him as definition and because his monologue's structure of reiterated ideas and images is dramatically convincing as meditation and deeply moving in meaning. The quiet, unostentatious, glowing intensity of the *Four Quartets* cannot be described but perhaps it can be illustrated.

This is the opening strophe of the first part of the final quartet, "Little Gidding."

> Midwinter spring is its own season
> Sempiternal though sodden towards sundown,
> Suspended in time, between pole and tropic.
> When the short day is brightest, with frost and fire,
> The brief sun flames the ice, on pond and ditches,
> In windless cold that is the heart's heat,
> Reflecting in a watery mirror
> A glare that is blindness in the early afternoon.
> And glow more intense than blaze of branch, or brazier,
> Stirs the dumb spirit: no wind, but pentecostal fire
> In the dark time of the year. Between melting and freezing
> The soul's sap quivers. There is no earth smell
> Or smell of living thing. This is the spring time
> But not in time's covenant. Now the hedgerow
> Is blanched for an hour with transitory blossom
> Of snow, a bloom more sudden
> Than that of summer, neither budding nor fading,
> Not in the scheme of generation.
> Where is the summer, the unimaginable
> Zero summer?

To this image of the seasonal world of time Mr. Eliot began to commit himself in *Ash-Wednesday,* not because the world of time is the whole of reality, but because "only through time time is conquered." What he is seeking is an image which will realize both the recognition that "in my beginning is my end" and the recognition that "in my end is my beginning." Only thus can he finally achieve "a sense of the timeless as well as of the temporal and of the timeless and temporal together," as he put it at the very beginning of his career.

This strophe is therefore first of all the description of a temporal occasion, what we sometimes call a spring*like* day in midwinter. But that language is false, for it recognizes only temporality, assumes that this is "really" only a midwinter moment that seems like spring. It is, of course, that; the *Quartets* do full justice to the world of time and recognize the intimacy within that world of man's life and nature's:

> Keeping the rhythm in their dancing
> As in their living in the living seasons
> The time of the seasons and the constellations
> The time of milking and the time of harvest
> The time of the coupling of man and woman
> And that of beasts. Feet rising and falling.
> Eating and drinking. Dung and death.

The modulation at the end of this passage from "East Coker" does not deny the reality of this life or its goodness; it only suggests the insufficiency of such a life.

If we recognize that the world of time is only a part of reality, then we recognize that this season is not merely spring*like.* Taken quite simply for what it appears, it is "its own season," namely, "midwinter spring." As such it is in fact "sempiternal"—only, to be sure, because time is real too, "sodden toward sundown." It is "suspended," but it is also "in time." The next two lines sustain this sense of our seasons' dual reality ("When the *short* day is *brightest*") and fix our attention on its special quality. This quality is hinted at by "Between pole and tropic"; it is made overt by "with frost and fire" and "The brief sun flames the ice."

But because men are always "living in the living seasons," this unseasonal season is, in both its temporality and its suspense, a season of the heart as well as a season of nature. "The brief sun flames the ice, on pond and ditches,/In windless cold that is the *heart's* heat." From this point on the strophe takes account of all these aspects of the season. For instance, "Reflecting in a watery mirror/A glare that is blindness in the early afternoon." This does complete justice to the temporal experience, the uneven reflecting surfaces of the ice, the merely uncomfortable glare of natural sunlight which, we remind ourselves, need be endured only for "the early afternoon." But it is also charged with an awareness that the uneven surface of man's nature has reflected a flash of the blinding glow that has, in the words of "Burnt Norton," "glittered out of the heart of light."

The emphasis in these first eight lines has been on the temporal phenomenon; the human one is largely implicit. The next four lines emphasize the human phenomenon, but keep the natural one before us by using the season of nature as a metaphor for the season of the heart ("Between melting and freezing/The soul's sap quivers"). The next seven lines generalize the image further. "This *is* the spring time," the spring time not of "time's covenant" but of timeless reality's, a spring which, if it stirs men's hearts more than the most vivid temporal passion, is also icy cold. It is hotter than "East Coker"'s rustic leaping through their bonfire in a commodious celebration of natural love but altogether without the smell of their mortality, the earthly smell of "dung and death."

The last two lines intensify our awareness that this is no mere description but an experience. In "Burnt Norton" the speaker had been impatient of mere time ("Ridiculous the waste sad time/Stretching before and after"); in "East Coker" he was still thinking almost entirely of "the intense moment/Isolated, with no before and after." But by "The Dry Salvages" he was aware that "the point of intersection of the timeless/With time, is an occupation for the saint": "for most of us, there is only the unattended/Moment, the moment in and out of time." In the last two lines of this strophe his anguished longing for the occupation of the saint reasserts itself. If midwinter spring can be what he has just experienced, what must the "unimaginable/Zero summer" be like, that inconceivable "time" when, simultaneously, midwinter has become zero weather and spring has become full summer?

Perhaps this illustration will suggest something of the quiet magnificence with which Mr. Eliot has finally brought together in the *Four Quartets* the two worlds which have lain apart in his imagination from the beginning of his career—the world of time and those who, like Sweeney, keep its rhythm, and the brilliant, ordered world of the disciplined imagination and those who, like the saints, keep its stillness. Here are Mr. Eliot's very great gifts at their best; much more, here is the reward for his having devoted a lifetime to the object he set himself at the beginning of his career, "to transmute his personal and private agonies into ... something universal and impersonal." If new readers are sometimes put off by the severity of Mr. Eliot's manners (as Mr. Eliot is himself when he rereads his early work) let them remember that without the intensity of will they indicate Mr. Eliot would never have been able to mix the desire of a brilliant midwestern Unitarian with the central memory of Western Culture and so show his time, not perhaps what it is, but what it would be if its nature were fully realized.

Ezra Pound

T. S. Eliot[1]

> *Il n'y a de livres que ceux où un écrivain s'est raconté lui-même en racontant les moeurs de ses contemporains—leurs rêves, leurs vanités, leurs amours, et leurs folies*—Rémy de Gourmont.

De Gourmont uses this sentence in writing of the incontestable superiority of *Madame Bovary, L'Education Sentimentale* and *Bouvard et Pécuchet* to *Salammbô* and *La Tentation de St Antoine.* A casual thought convinces one that it is true for all prose. Is it true also for poetry? One may give latitude to the interpretation of *rêves;* the gross public would have the poet write little else, but de Gourmont keeps a proportion. The vision should have its place in due setting if we are to believe its reality.

The few poems which Mr. Eliot has given us maintain this proportion, as they maintain other proportions of art. After much contemporary work that is merely factitious, much that is good in intention but impotently unfinished and incomplete, much whose flaws are due to sheer ignorance which a year's study or thought might have remedied, it is a comfort to come upon complete art, naïve despite its intellectual subtlety, lacking all pretense.

It is quite safe to compare Mr. Eliot's work with anything written in

[1]*Prufrock and Other Observations,* by T. S. Eliot. *The Egoist,* London. Essay first published in *Poetry,* 1917.

21

French, English or American since the death of Jules Laforgue. The
reader will find nothing better, and he will be extremely fortunate if he
finds much half as good.

The necessity, or at least the advisability, of comparing English or
American work with French work is not readily granted by the usual
English or American writer. If you suggest it, the Englishman answers
that he has not thought about it—he does not see why he should bother
himself about what goes on south of the channel; the American replies
by stating that you are "no longer American." This is the bitterest jibe
in his vocabulary. The net result is that it is extremely difficult to read
one's contemporaries. After a time one tires of "promise."

I should like the reader to note how complete is Mr. Eliot's
depiction of our contemporary condition. He has not confined himself
to genre or to society portraiture. His

> lonely men in shirt-sleeves leaning out of windows

are as real as his ladies who

> come and go
> Talking of Michelangelo.

His "one-night cheap hotels" are as much "there" as are his

> four wax candles in the darkened room,
> Four rings of light upon the ceiling overhead,
> An atmosphere of Juliet's tomb.

And, above all, there is no rhetoric, although there is Elizabethan
reading in the background. Were I a French critic, skilled in their
elaborate art of writing books about books, I should probably go to
some length discussing Mr. Eliot's two sorts of metaphor: his wholly
unrealizable, always apt, half ironic suggestion, and his precise realiz-
able picture. It would be possible to point out his method of conveying
a whole situation and half a character by three words of a quoted
phrase; his constant aliveness; his mingling of a very subtle observation
with the unexpectedness of a backhanded cliché. It is, however,
extremely dangerous to point out such devices. The method is Mr.
Eliot's own, but as soon as one has reduced even a fragment of it to
formula, someone else, not Mr. Eliot, someone else wholly lacking in
his aptitudes, will at once try to make poetry by mimicking his external

procedure. And this indefinite "someone" will, needless to say, make a botch of it.

For what the statement is worth, Mr. Eliot's work interests me more than that of any other poet now writing in English.[2] The most interesting poems in Victorian English are Browning's *Men and Women,* or, if that statement is too absolute, let me contend that the form of these poems is the most vital form of that period of English, and that the poems written in that form are the least like each other in content. Antiquity gave us Ovid's *Heroides* and Theocritus' woman using magic. The form of Browning's *Men and Women* is more alive than the epistolary form of the *Heroides.* Browning included a certain amount of ratiocination and of purely intellectual comment, and in just that proportion he lost intensity. Since Browning there have been very few good poems of this sort. Mr. Eliot has made two notable additions to the list. And he has placed his people in contemporary settings, which is much more difficult than to render them with medieval romantic trappings. If it is permitted to make comparison with a different art, let me say that he has used contemporary detail very much as Velasquez used contemporary detail in *Las Meninas;* the cold gray-green tones of the Spanish painter have, it seems to me, an emotional value not unlike the emotional value of Mr. Eliot's rhythms, and of his vocabulary.

James Joyce has written the best novel of my decade, and perhaps the best criticism of it has come from a Belgian who said, "All this is as true of my country as of Ireland." Eliot has a like ubiquity of application. Art does not avoid universals, it strikes at them all the harder in that it strikes through particulars. Eliot's work rests apart from that of the many new writers who have used the present freedoms to no advantage, who have gained no new precision of language, and no variety in their cadence. His men in shirt-sleeves, and his society ladies, are not a local manifestation; they are the stuff of our modern world, and true of more countries than one. I would praise the work for its fine tone, its humanity, and its realism; for all good art is realism of one sort or another.

It is complained that Eliot is lacking in emotion. "La Figlia che Piange" is an adequate confutation.

If the reader wishes mastery of "regular form" the *Conversation Galante* is sufficient to show that symmetrical form is within Mr. Eliot's grasp. You will hardly find such neatness save in France; such modern neatness, save in Laforgue.

[2] A.D. 1917.

De Gourmont's phrase to the contrary notwithstanding, the supreme test of a book is that we should feel some unusual intelligence working behind the words. By this test various other new books, that I have, or might have, beside me, go to pieces. The barrels of sham poetry that every decade and school and fashion produce, go to pieces. It is sometimes extremely difficult to find any other particular reason for their being so unsatisfactory. I have expressly written here not "intellect" but "intelligence." There is no intelligence without emotion. The emotion may be anterior or concurrent. There may be emotion without much intelligence, but that does not concern us.

VERSIFICATION

A conviction as to the rightness or wrongness of *vers libre* is no guarantee of a poet. I doubt if there is much use trying to classify the various kinds of *vers libre,* but there is an anarchy which may be vastly overdone; and there is a monotony of bad usage as tiresome as any typical eighteenth or nineteenth century flatness.

In a recent article Mr. Eliot contended, or seemed to contend, that good *vers libre* was little more than a skillful evasion of the better known English meters. His article was defective in that he omitted all consideration of meters depending on quantity, alliteration, etc.; in fact, he wrote as if all meters were measured by accent. This may have been tactful on his part, it may have brought his article nearer to the comprehension of his readers (that is, those of the *New Statesman* people chiefly concerned with the sociology of the "button" and "unit" variety). But he came nearer the fact when he wrote elsewhere: "No *vers* is *libre* for the man who wants to do a good job."

Alexandrine and other grammarians have made cubby-holes for various groupings of syllables; they have put names upon them, and have given various labels to "meters" consisting of combinations of these different groups.[3] Thus it would be hard to escape contact with some group or other; only an encyclopedist could ever be half sure he had done so. The known categories would allow a fair liberty to the most conscientious traditionalist. The most fanatical vers-librist will escape them with difficulty. However, I do not think there is any crying need for verse with absolutely no rhythmical basis.

On the other hand, I do not believe that Chopin wrote to a

---

[3] A.D. 1940. Prosody is the articulation of the total sound of a poem. E.P.

metronome. There is undoubtedly a sense of music that takes count of the "shape" of the rhythm in a melody rather than of bar divisions, which came rather late in the history of written music and were certainly not the first or most important thing that musicians attempted to record. The creation of such shapes is part of thematic invention. Some musicians have the faculty of invention, rhythmic, melodic. Likewise some poets.

Treatises full of musical notes and of long and short marks have never been convincingly used. Find a man with thematic invention and all he can say is that he gets what the Celts call a "chune" in his head, and that the words "go into it," or when they don't "go into it" they "stick out and worry him."

You can not force a person to play a musical masterpiece correctly, even by having the notes "correctly" printed on the paper before him; neither can you force a person to feel the movement of poetry, be the meter "regular" or "irregular." I have heard Mr. Yeats trying to read Burns, struggling in vain to fit the *Birks o' Aberfeldy* and *Bonnie Alexander* into the mournful keen of the *Wind among the Reeds.* Even in regular meters there are incompatible systems of music.

I have heard the best orchestral conductor in England read poems in free verse, poems in which the rhythm was so faint as to be almost imperceptible. He[4] read them with the author's cadence, with flawless correctness. A distinguished statesman[5] read from the same book with the intonations of a legal document, paying no attention to the movement inherent in the words before him. I have heard a celebrated Dante scholar and medieval enthusiast read the sonnets of the *Vita Nuova* as if they were not only prose, but the ignominious prose of a man devoid of emotions: an utter castration.

The leader of orchestra said to me, "There is more for a musician in a few lines with something rough or uneven, such as Byron's

> There be nothing of Beauty's daughters
> With a magic like thee;

than in whole pages of regular poetry."

Unless a man can put some thematic invention into *vers libre,* he would perhaps do well to stick to "regular" meters, which have certain chances of being musical from their form, and certain other chances of

---

[4] Beecham (E.P.).
[5] Birrell (E.P.).

being musical through his failure in fitting the form. In *vers libre* his musical chances are but in sensitivity and invention.

Mr. Eliot is one of the very few who have given a personal rhythm, an identifiable quality of sound as well as of style. And at any rate, his book is the best thing in poetry since . . . (for the sake of peace I will leave that date to the imagination). I have read most of the poems many times; I have read the whole book at breakfast time and from flimsy proof-sheets: I believe these are "test conditions." And, "confound it, the fellow can write."

Bernard Bergonzi

T. S. Eliot: The Early Poems

"Portrait of a Lady" and "Prufrock" are dramatic monologues where the drifting invertebrate reflections of Laforgue's *Dernier Vers* are given a certain stiffening and verbal energy by the influence of late-Elizabethan and Jacobean dramatic verse. "Portrait of a Lady," written when Eliot was twenty-one, is his first important poem and one which remains impressive; it is in no sense a piece of apprentice work. It is more immediately approachable than "Prufrock" and makes the best possible introduction to the study of Eliot's poetic *oeuvre*. The title recalls Henry James, and though there is nothing of Isabel Archer in the poem, the situation and atmosphere have some of the quality of a James short story dealing in muted desperation and polite betrayal. Conrad Aiken has referred to its source in Eliot's socializing in Boston and Cambridge: "our dear deplorable friend, Miss X, the *précieuse ridicule* to end all preciosity, serving tea so exquisitely among her bric-a-brac, was to be pinned like a butterfly to a page in 'Portrait of a Lady.' " There is little in the poem that will seem strange to a reader familiar with Browning's dramatic monologues; though it makes an immediate contrast with the typical form of the latter, in which an articulate, even garrulous, speaker steadily reveals himself in his remarks to an interlocutor whose own remarks are never heard. In Eliot's poem, which might be called a "dramatic interior monologue," the lady does most of the talking and the young man silently ruminates pursuing the aimless reflection that flickers through his consciousness. There is a carefully composed time scheme, with episodes in December, April, and

October, providing an early example of Eliot's lifelong preoccupation
with times and seasons. The characters emerge from their broken and
unsatisfactory encounters with a fair degree of solidity and identity;
they exist in a world which, however precarious it may be, has a certain
coherence. The lady's speeches combine the formal and the colloquial
with an impelling nervous energy. They indicate the presence of the
potential dramatist in Eliot in a way that does not reappear until "A
Game of Chess" in *The Waste Land;* there is a remarkable virtuosity in
the counterpointing of the marked yet wavering rhythm, the tones of
the speaking voice, and the intricate syntax.

In one respect, "Portrait of a Lady" is as much novelistic as it is
dramatic. We never know the situation "as it is," but through the
consciousness of the young man who not only renders what happened
but tries, however inadequately, to justify his attitudes and at the same
time unconsciously reveals his own moral hollowness. This device is
known to the critics of fiction as the "corrupt" or "deluded" narrator,
and James's *Aspern Papers* offers a good example of it. In Eliot's poem
the narrator's consciousness is at all times on the verge of dissolution:
his attempts to engage in polite drawing-room conversation are inter-
fered with by the grotesque musical sounds going on inside his head.
(Eliot may be parodying the symbolist insistence that music is the
highest of the arts.) He makes an effort literally to compose himself but
his impressions remain as fragmentary and disjunctive as the items in a
daily paper, though his consciousness is haunted by possibilities of
aesthetic and moral significance that remain beyond him:

> I take my hat: how can I make a cowardly amends
> For what she has said to me?
> You will see me any morning in the park
> Reading the comics and the sporting page.
> Particularly I remark
> An English countess goes upon the stage.
> A Greek was murdered at a Polish dance,
> Another bank defaulter has confessed.
> I keep my countenance,
> I remain self-possessed
> Except when a street-piano, mechanical and tired
> Reiterates some worn-out common song
> With the smell of hyacinths across the garden
> Recalling things that other people have desired.
> Are these ideas right or wrong?

F. R. Leavis has rightly praised these lines, remarking that "the play of tone and inflection means the possibility of a kind of strong and subtle thinking in poetry"; they show to what extent Eliot was an innovative force in the poetry of 1910. They also point to elements in his later poetry, such as the drifting cosmopolitans of "Gerontion" and *The Waste Land,* and the wistful eroticism symbolized by the Hyacinth Girl.

In the third section of "Portrait of a Lady" the narrator seems reduced, even in his own estimation, to a state of subhuman absurdity: "I mount the stairs and turn the handle of the door/And feel as if I had mounted on my hands and knees." The possibility of disintegration becomes palpable. In the closing lines the possibility of the lady's death presents him with an image of significance that he can neither fully grasp nor brush aside, though the act of contemplating it at least restores his consciousness to a momentary coherence. (The line, "Well! and what if she should die some afternoon," shows Eliot boldly enlarging on a Laforguian source, "Enfin, si, par un soir, elle meurt dans mes livres. . . .")

There are obvious things in common between "Portrait of a Lady" and "The Love Song of J. Alfred Prufrock"; both, for example, employ the Laforguian dramatic monologue, unfolding the fragmentary consciousness of a male narrator who recoils from or is otherwise unable to accomplish a possible sexual encounter. Yet "Prufrock" is considerably more radical. If "Portrait of a Lady" is like a painting that, though stylized, is basically representational, "Prufrock" is like a cubist version of a similar subject. The time, place, and identity which were genuinely if precariously present in the earlier poem have all been dissolved.

The name "Prufrock," which occurs only in the title, is derived, as Hugh Kenner has pointed out, from a firm of furniture wholesalers in St. Louis in the early years of the century. Like so many other fragments of casual experience it remained lodged in Eliot's memory until it could be put to some good use. In the full title of the poem, the conventional expectations of "Love Song" are instantly and sharply counteracted by the absurd proper name that follows. It is an effective example in miniature of Eliot's method which has several times given a strangely ghostly identity to bare, unqualified names. The poem's epigraph is from Dante, the first of many such quotations and allusions in Eliot's work; it is hard to exaggerate Eliot's indebtedness, and the extent to which he has aspired to identify himself with Dante, though the aspiration, it must be emphasized, arises from profound differences in temperament and situation. The quotation is from *Inferno* XXVII, and the words are spoken by Guido da Montefeltro: "If I thought my answer were to one who ever could return to the world, this flame should shake no more; but since none ever did return alive from this depth, if what I hear be true, without fear of infamy I answer thee." By the time we reach the opening lines of the poem itself the implication is plain: this is hell and there is no possibility of escaping from it. Indeed, the first words, "Let us go then, you and I," recall the many passages in which Virgil gently urges Dante on in their journey through the *Inferno* and *Purgatorio*. These opening lines are already some of the best known in English poetry. The way in which these, and so many other of his lines, etch themselves ineradicably into the memory is a sign of Eliot's genius as a poet (and this, it should be added, is something quite different from the mechanical memorability of mnemonics and jingles).

> Let us go then, you and I,
> When the evening is spread out against the sky
> Like a patient etherised upon a table;

These lines have their own bizarre beauty and, as Eliot once claimed about poetry in general, can be appreciated before they are fully understood. Indeed, it is precisely in their efforts to understand these lines, and everything that follows, that so many readers of the poem go astray. There was a time when it was believed that because of Eliot's interest in the Metaphysical poets, such strange similes as this were really examples of the "metaphysical conceit"; yet this belief is a delusion. The conceit depended for its effect on the sudden sharp realization of an intellectually coherent resemblance between elements of experience that seem at first sight quite disconnected. In Eliot's poem it is not possible to see any way in which the evening is really like a patient etherized upon a table, or in which the fog resembles a domestic animal wandering outside a house. The similes remain powerful; but the appropriate question to ask is, What kind of consciousness is it that sees the world in such terms? Similarly, a great deal of energy has been misapplied in trying to extract a "story" from "Prufrock," and in working out who the characters are, and what time scheme is involved. It is as futile to do this as to try to trace elements of photographic likeness or "correct" perspective in, say, Picasso's *Demoiselles d'Avignon,* a work which has an innovative importance similar to that of Eliot's poem.

"Prufrock" offers not a verifiable account of the world, nor the unfolding revelation of a "real" character, but rather, as Hugh Kenner has said, "a zone of consciousness" which each reader has to pass through for himself and which may not present itself to the same reader in identical terms on successive readings. If Prufrock has an analogue in previous literature, it is to be found in Frédéric Moreau, the aloof and timorous hero of Flaubert's *L'Education Sentimentale,* a novel for which Eliot had an intense admiration. In his essay on Ben Jonson he writes of Frédéric:

> He is constructed partly by negative definition, built up by a great number of observations. We cannot isolate him from the environment in which we find him; it may be an environment which is or can be much universalized; nevertheless it, and the figure in it, consist of very many observed particular facts, the actual world. Without this world the figure dissolves.

For all the vividness with which the poem presents notations of an urban scene and a trivial social world, it is impossible to say which of these elements are externally "there" and which are the *disjecta membra* of a disordered consciousness. The reader has to make, provisionally perhaps, many decisions for himself; as a major work in the symbolist manner, "Prufrock" forces the reader into a collaboratively creative role. Yet within its enveloping "zone of consciousness" certain elements are unmistakable. We are involved, whether we like it or not, in a dual sense of boredom at the inauthenticities of a predictable social round ("I have measured out my life with coffee spoons") and of terror at the sexual undercurrents in such a life. And in "Prufrock" the hints of dehumanization in "Portrait of a Lady" are made explicit.

In the following lines we see a convergence of the poem's main themes, or obsessions. "Eyes" were to become a dominant motif in Eliot's poetry, and in this passage we notice his inclination toward the French fashion of using impersonally the definite article with parts of the body, thereby fragmenting any sense of personal identity:

> And I have known the eyes already, known them all—
> The eyes that fix you in a formulated phrase,
> And when I am formulated, sprawling on a pin,
> When I am pinned and wriggling on the wall,
> Then how should I begin
> To spit out all the butt-ends of my days and ways?

"Prufrock," as Hugh Kenner has said, offers not a character but "a name plus a Voice." The name is unforgettable and the Voice, as it meditates calmly on tedium and terror and further possibilities of disintegration—"I should have been a pair of ragged claws/Scuttling across the floors of silent seas"—nevertheless impresses us as a strong and finely articulate voice. In this respect, "Prufrock" offers a remarkable anticipation of Samuel Beckett's late fiction. Whatever chaos of feelings gives rise to Eliot's early poetry—and what may begin as an adolescent nervousness about sex is soon transformed into metaphysical dread—the power of language never fails to offer order and consolation, even though, in "Prufrock," the order is constantly on the verge of disintegration.

Many years later Eliot wrote "In my end is my beginning," and, as I have suggested, there is no coherent time sequence in "The Love Song of J. Alfred Prufrock." The voice goes on calmly recording or anticipating decisions and indecisions, disasters and recoveries, and by the time we reach the end of the poem it is impossible to say whether we have made any progress at all in time and action from the opening lines. The process could in fact continue almost indefinitely, or so it seems, at least until we reach the celebrated line, so Tennysonian in its plangency, "I shall wear the bottoms of my trousers rolled," which seems to point to a fresh variation on a theme rather than any sense of finality. Yet Eliot must end the poem at some point, and he does so with lines that for all their beauty might have come from a different and more conventional poem: the nervous sexuality of a small world of novels and teacups and skirts that trail along the floor is exchanged for the pure but remote eroticism of the "sea-girls wreathed with seaweed red and brown." The last line, with its ambivalent suggestions both of waking and drowning, offers an eventual possibility of escaping—despite the message of the epigraph—from one of the most intense, yet controlled, immersions in extreme experience in modern literature.

Regarded as a whole, "Prufrock" shows both the characteristic limitations of Eliot's imagination and his equally characteristic power of overcoming them. It is a matter of record that the final version of the poem was assembled in 1911 from a number of sections written over the past year; in a letter written to Harriet Monroe in 1915, Ezra Pound remarked of "Prufrock": "I dislike the paragraph about Hamlet, but it is an early and cherished bit and T. E. won't give it up. . . ." And what is true of "Prufrock" is also true of most of Eliot's other major poems: *The Waste Land,* "The Hollow Men," *Ash-Wednesday,* and "Burnt Norton" were all put together out of fragments, in some cases written over a period of years and known to have previously existed in

other combinations. In 1956 Eliot remarked that "poetic originality is
largely an original way of assembling the most disparate and unlikely
material to make a new whole." A traditionally minded reader might
well regard "Prufrock" as "formless," whereas a sympathetic reader
would rightly say that its form was musical rather than that of a
preexisting literary mode. It is less often remarked, though I think it is
true, that the forms of T. S. Eliot's major poems do not inevitably
exclude other possible arrangements of their constituent fragments.

For Eliot, I suggest, experience presented itself in an intensely
realized but disparate series of elements. And there was no possibility
of organizing them into larger structures by the power of the rational
intellect or by relying on familiar literary forms. Nevertheless, Eliot did
possess an extraordinary ability, that seems to have existed below the
level of conscious experience, of synthesizing his fragmentary perceptions. One senses it in the strong yet immensely subtle sense of rhythm
that gives his poems their particular power; and it is a rhythm that
seems to go deeper than mere aural values. The late Anton Ehrenzweig,
in his fascinating book, *The Hidden Order of Art,* refers to "an ego
rhythm that underlies all creative work" and some such quality seems
obscurely to have fused the constituent elements in Eliot's poetry, just
as it does in the juxtaposed heterogeneous forms, or *collage* composi-
tions, of many modern painters. Such an "ego rhythm" is by definition
wholly personal and represents a form of calligraphy, where a man's
signature is unmistakably his own, but never "inevitably" so, since no
two signatures will be absolutely identical. This kind of form, though
real enough, is far less tangible than the classical precepts absorbed
from Irving Babbit and other conservative masters, and may help to
explain why Eliot regarded the act of creation as a surrender to obscure
and possibly dangerous forces. In *The Sacred Wood* he praised Dante
for "the most comprehensive, and the most *ordered* presentation of
emotions that has ever been made." Such an order, which in the *Divine
Comedy* is simultaneously moral, intellectual, and aesthetic, was not
within Eliot's compass as an artist, however much he may have valued it
as a critic. It is this, I think, which explains the peculiar intensity of
Eliot's attachment to Dante, the poet who dominated his *oeuvre,* from
the words of Guido da Montefeltro at the beginning of "Prufrock" to
the superb Dantesque re-creation in "Little Gidding."

The four "Preludes," written in 1910 and 1911, dwell on the same
low aspects of urban life that we see depicted in "Prufrock." The first
two present a purely "objective" rendering of the city at evening and
morning—small-scale equivalents, as E. D. H. Greene has suggested, of

Baudelaire's "Crépuscule du Soir" and "Crépuscule du Matin"—and are in effect perfect Imagist poems, written before Ezra Pound sponsored an Imagist movement in London in 1912. Hugh Kenner has denied the Imagist element in the "Preludes," saying that they are haunted by the need for an absent significance, whereas the Imagists relied simply on the self-sufficient presentation of an object. Whatever their precepts may have been, it seems to me that in practice the best Imagist poems, like Pound's "Dans le Metro" or "Fan piece for her imperial lord," do reach after human significance. "Preludes" I and II are examples of a kind of urban poetry that had existed fitfully in England since the middle of the nineteenth century. One can recall Tennyson's superb stanza from "In Memoriam":

> He is not here; but far away
>   The noise of life begins again,
>   And ghastly thro' the drizzling rain
> On the bald street breaks the blank day.

And there are some interesting examples written in the nineties, under the direct influence of Baudelaire. The first line of "Preludes" II, "The morning comes to consciousness," shows Eliot's conviction, so fully expressed in "Portrait of a Lady" and "Prufrock," that the objects of perception, for all our attempts at objectivity, can never be wholly separated from the mind that perceives. In "Preludes" III and IV he makes explicit the mind's yearning for significance beyond the random content of consciousness, presented in cubist disjunctiveness:

> And short square fingers stuffing pipes,
> And evening newspapers, and eyes
> Assured of certain certainties.

Hence the wistful aspiration for "such a vision of the street/As the street hardly understands" or "The notion of some infinitely gentle/ Infinitely suffering thing."

"Preludes" contain some of the most memorable epiphanies of urban experience in English, and the city is shown as essentially anonymous. Yet it is interesting to note that the early drafts of these poems, contained in a leather-bound notebook in the Berg Collection at the New York Public Library (which also includes drafts of several other poems written at this time, so far unpublished), referred specifically to parts of Boston in their titles; it was a happy decision of Eliot's to delete them before publishing the poems, thereby leaving them a wide range of potential reference.

"Rhapsody on a Windy Night," a product of Eliot's stay in Paris, also explores a gloomy urban environment, though a more definably French one. Phrases drawn from Laforgue are combined with others from Baudelaire and Charles-Louis Philippe; and some commentators have seen in the phrase "Dissolve the floors of memory" evidence of Bergsonian influence. The "Rhapsody" is a unique poem in Eliot's work: a record, as it seems, of a noctambulistic movement through city streets, which presents the contents of memory in bizarre images with many dream-like juxtapositions. The flux of time is divided by the chiming of the hours, a precarious and arbitrary imposition of order. The poem is intensely and characteristically visual; there are several instances of Eliot's obsessive image of eyes and an imagistic concentration on objects that dwells, as a painter might, on their quiddity while hinting at their larger implications. The "Rhapsody" is visual in its detail and musical in its organization, a pure example of the "music of images," to use a somewhat overworked phrase. It is, I think, a superb poem in a vein that Eliot did not follow up: possibly it involved a degree of symbolist remoteness from the discursive that Eliot, for all his preference for music over statement, was disinclined to accept.

There remains, from the first phase of Eliot's poetry, "La Figlia che Piange," which was written after his return to Harvard. This poem was an early favorite of conventionally minded readers and anthologists, for whom its fairly straightforward lyricism was in agreeable contrast to the radical imagery and associations of Eliot's other poems. As a result, it assumed for a time the kind of place in Eliot's career that "The Lake Isle of Innisfree" did in Yeats's or "The Goodly Fere" in Pound's, to his understandable dissatisfaction. It has worn less well than "Prufrock" and the others, though it is technically adroit in the way it blends Pre-Raphaelite imagery and plangency of sound with Eliot's characteristically nervous subtlety of rhythm. F. R. Leavis has lately argued that the excellence of this poem lies in "love unequivocally presented, love that calls for lyrical expression—the poem is unique in the Eliot volume." It is, however, scarcely unequivocal; the poem is, in fact, an essay in Laforguian evasiveness, where the relation between the narrator and the male lover is extremely ambiguous, and one is no more sure than in "Prufrock" of the objective pattern of events. To my mind, there is a certain suggestion of a scene being set up for voyeuristic contemplation: the thematic affinity with "Prufrock" is closer than one might imagine. And while acknowledging the direct though rather formal lyricism of the first part of the poem, one also has to notice the carefully distancing diction in the final lines, where the ironic mode reasserts itself. Nevertheless, it is worth remarking that Eliot did not use the recurring "staircase" image in such an elevated way again until *Ash-Wednesday*.

The poems of 1910-1912 were the first and unmistakable signs of Eliot's genius; some aspects of them were to develop throughout his poetic career while others remained undeveloped. They also contain characteristics that have frequently troubled critics. One of them concerns Eliot's use of literary sources, for which he is still sometimes accused of plagiarism. One can say briefly that Eliot was not, in principle, doing anything different from Chaucer or Spenser or even Shakespeare, all of whom made free use of foreign sources for their own good ends, though Eliot admittedly drew on a more eclectic and obscure range of writers than they did. Eliot's use of French Symbolist poetry was essential for him in the formation of a language: in general he used foreign poets to help him understand and express his own experience, rather than in any jackdaw-like search for exotic beauties. Eliot's use of other literature was more existential and less purely aesthetic than Pound's, despite the similarity of their approaches.

Again, Eliot's early poems clearly manifest an intense sense of erotic failure and bewilderment; there is no point in denying that much of the motivating force of his poetry arises from an unhappy sexual obsession. He was not, if one wants to use such a phrase, "on the side of Life," and for this he has been regularly called to account, perhaps more in sorrow than in anger, by many critics in whom an orthodoxy of sexual fulfillment proves just as tyrannical as religious orthodoxies were for earlier generations. If Eliot expressed such failures in his poetry and tried to come to terms with them, then he was in fact expressing a perennial aspect of the human condition, however unfashionable it may be to recognize the fact.

M. L. Rosenthal

The Waste Land *as an Open Structure*

The recovery of the lost version of *The Waste Land*—"the original drafts including the annotations of Ezra Pound" reproduced in the Valerie Eliot edition of 1971—compels a new recognition of the open character of the poem's structure. I do not mean that the earlier version shows us what Eliot was "really" doing in the later one; only the text a poet finally decides on takes the responsibility for itself. But because of certain different emphases while the poem was still in the making, the sense of improvisation at the high pitch of genius that struck the first reader of the printed text is reinforced. One almost does well to forget Pound and think of someone as unlikely as Lawrence, with his idea of Whitman as the poet of the "open road," and of a poetry "of the present"; Lawrence wrote in 1918 of "the poetry of that which is at hand: the immediate present. In the immediate present there is no perfection, no consummation, nothing finished. The strands are all flying, quivering, intermingling into the web, the waters are shaking the moon. . . . This is the unrestful, ungraspable poetry of the sheer present, poetry whose very permanency lies in its wind-like transit. Whitman's is the best poetry of this kind." This was in Lawrence's introduction to the American edition of his *New Poems.* But five years earlier still he had written, in a letter: "I have always tried to get an emotion out in its own course, without altering it. It needs the finest instinct imaginable, much finer than the skill of craftsmen."

Reprinted by permission from Mosaic, 6 *(Fall, 1972), 181-189. Copyright © 1972 by The Editors,* Mosaic, *The University of Manitoba Press.*

One could assemble a huge battery of statements by Lawrence and others, even by Pound and Eliot, to show how much a renewed fascination with the organic and "wind-harp" conceptions of Romantic poetics affected the young advance-guard poets and theorists of the time. Even those who made something of a show of their intellectual rigor—their learning and "classicism" and formal self-discipline—were infected with this desire to write directly out of the "immediate present," to use the language and the experience and the whole context of life that was "at hand." To isolate, release, recognize, and ride the real emotional direction of the poem—such an aim involves the sense of improvisation at the pitch of genius that I have mentioned. The true poem, in this perspective, consists of a series of affects that together create the life of the poem; their order is a tentative satisfying of the need to explore the emotional range they embody that is felt by the poem's ultimate sensibility or speaking voice. It is interesting that Eliot, in the face of his poem's obvious preoccupations with large moral, religious, and social issues and with philosophical and cultural meanings of a very inclusive kind, should have remarked that "to me it was only the relief of a personal and wholly insignificant grouse against life; it is just a piece of rhythmic grumbling."[1] It was not that those broad and deep preoccupations, which enable us to see a certain clear rhetorical order in the progression of the poem, are not actually present. But they are present as dimensions of a speaking consciousness, rather than as the main point or purpose of the poem. Eliot himself, in his doctoral dissertation, had concerned himself with F. H. Bradley's concept of "Immediate Experience" as the ambiguous, undifferentiated condition of the living self in the midst of its world but hardly sorted out from the reality that engulfs and saturates it.

The context of Bradleyan thought brought to bear on the sensibility that broods over the shifting moments of *The Waste Land* has been discussed by a number of scholars. Eliot spells the key-formulation out for us by quoting directly, in his notes, from Bradley's *Appearance and Reality*:

> My external sensations are no less private to myself than are my thoughts and my feelings. In either case my experience falls within my own circle, a circle closed on the outside; and, with all its elements alike, every sphere is opaque to the others which surround it. . . . In brief, regarded as an existence which appears in a soul, the whole world for each is peculiar and private to that soul.

[1] Quoted in the Valerie Eliot edition, p. xxiii.

The passage is applied directly, of course, to lines 412-417 of *The Waste Land*, in which the isolation of the speaking self by pride and by failure of sympathy is presented as a hapless condition after all.

> I have heard the key
> Turn in the door once and turn once only
> We think of the key, each in his prison
> Thinking of the key, each confirms a prison
> Only at nightfall, aethereal rumours
> Revive for a moment a broken Coriolanus

Eliot refers us as well to *Inferno*, xxxiii, 46, the point at which Ugolino, imprisoned with his sons in the Tower of Hunger, awakes to find they are being sealed into their prison. The relevance of one motif of tragic isolation to another is obvious, though the full hideousness of the Ugolino tale can hardly be assumed to be evoked in Eliot's lines through the mediation of a footnote (especially since the allusion to Coriolanus in the passage itself takes us in a quite different direction). The Bradleyan approach, indeed, implies for the poet a continuously depressive condition that was not at all the concern of the philosopher: That state in which the psyche is so invaded and possessed by "outside" reality that it cannot define itself and its purposes in any actively formed perspective.

Poetically speaking, this is the state of readiness shared by the poet and his work—readiness to receive the unavoidable impact of reality and readiness to move out of this open and vulnerable position into the exploration of possible new sets of attitude and awareness. The characteristic lyric poem of the past two centuries begins with recognition of a real situation that has perhaps elusively melancholy overtones, or with a direct statement of a feeling of sadness or of precarious balance. It moves into a sense of the complexity of the relationships and feelings it is contemplating, often marked by a sense of confusion and of the breaking down of normal distinctions. It ends with something like reconciliation, but on closer observation the reconciliation consists in the speaker's recognition of a drastically and tragically unchangeable reality. Paradoxically, this recognition has the ring of a joyous affirmation. Eliot's "Shantih shantih shantih," which picks up from the gloriously elated language of ascetic abnegation in lines 419-423 ("The boat responded/Gaily" etc.), is but one of a very long series that would include such endings as Wallace Stevens's "Downward to darkness on extended wings" and Yeats's

Hermits upon Mount Meru or Everest,
Caverned in night under the drifted snow,
Or where that snow and winter's dreadful blast
Beat down upon their naked bodies, know
That day brings round the night, that before dawn
His glory and his monument are gone

The movement, in other words, is from a state of depressive awareness to one of depressive transcendence. It is not usually a straight-line movement, particularly in a sequence; except in relatively short pieces, it tends to be a series of balancings, in which the depressive state inseparable from a sufficiently open sensitivity is countered by momentary holdings against the chaos threatening the speaker both from without and from within. A lyric poem is in this way of seeing it a sensibility in motion. The motion is toward a tentative reconciliation by way of a number of poised balancings interspersed among movements of loss and dissolution. These balancings hold off absolute loss of morale, if only through the purity with which a negative recognition is evoked and sustained. Let us again cite lines 412-417, both because we have already noted the Bradleyan reference attached to it and because it is a strategically placed passage. It presents sharp and striking images for the speaker's sense of spiritual isolation and self-defeated pride; at the same time, it has positive tonalities mostly contradicted by the literal context. I say "mostly" because the image of a key that locks one into oneself does not exclude the possibility of the key's being turned the other way, and because there are associations of transcendence and tragic heroism implicit in the thought of "aetherial rumours" that "revive" even for only "a moment" even a "broken Coriolanus." This is a balancing, though on the whole negative in its implications. Another "positive" tonality is created by the word "confirms," though what is being confirmed is "a prison." The music of the passage sustains its balancing of motifs and tones. The confessional voice at the start, followed by the meditative voice that shifts from "I" to "we" and then by the exalted melancholy of the closing two lines, introduces a play on the word "key" that induces contemplation of its varied suggestiveness partly through sheer repetition and partly because it is alliterative with "confirms" and "Coriolanus" and has an insistent vowel echoed in "we" and in "aetherial." By the time the passage concludes we are thinking of "keys" to the poem's psychological frustrations and to its largest possible meanings as against the dead pressure of a continuum of undifferentiated reality.[2]

In its formal movement the passage epitomizes *The Waste Land* as a whole. Its final balance is not really final at all; it is a precarious stay only against breakdown, a set of notes that might easily enough be extended with other groupings of images—as in fact the next six lines do brilliantly, and as the next eleven lines, which end the poem, do once again. Those final eleven lines, too, "handle" the problem that was projected at the very beginning of the poem by jumbling together the basic tonalities of morale that punctuate the whole poem. These are, in order of appearance, the breakdown in madness and meaninglessness that comes with loss of sustaining vision, the passion to search out purification by discipline and mortification, the inseparable linking of tragedy and transporting desire in mythical and literary tradition, the emptiness felt by the speaker himself (coming forward, at last, as the poet who has "shored" the "fragments" of which the poem is made "against my ruins"), and the counter-motifs of spiritual redemption and calm at the end, themselves concealed as nonsense words until the English-speaking reader is properly indoctrinated.

The poem no more necessarily ends here than if it were one of Pound's *Cantos*. The real movement of *The Waste Land* is of brief, irregularly alternating cycles of depressive letdown and of resistance to it. As Lawrence said he tried to do, Eliot "gets an emotion out in its own course, without altering it"; he lets himself be carried by it but improvises ways of coping with it, for the "emotion" is actually a complex of feelings and attitudes informing what Eliot downgraded, half-humorously, as the "personal and wholly insignificant grouse against life" that he used the poem to "relieve."

Not to go into too tedious detail, we may trace the alternations of affect that define the progress of "The Burial of the Dead," and then add a few notes about later sections. The exquisite and poignant music of the first four lines, with their vital and painful challenge to meet the self-renewing demands of life, has a curious echo without resonance in the ensuing three lines. These are deliberately dulled and casually diffident in tone though they sustain the participial rhyming and general rhythmic character of the opening. Marie's expanded, more

---

[2] See Richard Wollheim's excellent "Eliot and F. H. Bradley: An Account," in *Eliot in Perspective: A Symposium*, ed. Graham Martin (New York: Humanities Press, 1970). Wollheim takes up this passage, but without regard to its poetic character.

relaxed lines provide another kind of echo of the opening. Memory and desire are evoked once more, but are rendered trivial by the life-patterns within which they are held; loose rhythm of the opening of this section, and the anticlimactic ending, make Marie's speech that of one of the dull roots of lines 4-7. If one still feels a certain bravery and touching love of excitement in what she says, the deeper voice of lines 19-30, turning on such roots and branches as could possibly grow "out of this stony rubbish," introduces the sound of prophetic horror at human reality seen in its terrifying amoral emptiness. The new voice's compulsive repetitions balance this terror at our loss against the promise of a revelation that may be yet more terrible. Then the music of rhetorical prophetic insistence drops away. It was another reverberation, we should note, of the atmosphere of challenge suggested in the opening lines, and even of their romantic intensity. But now something more similarly evocative of the world of erotic desire and its full implication of painful self-awareness re-enters the poem in the lines from Tristan und Isolde and in the "hyacinth girl" passage. Madame Sosostris, another dull root, presents a welcome comic and satiric variation while introducing themes from the deeper world of prophetic mystery though she does not understand them. At last, in its turn, the "Unreal City" passage (one of the three or four most powerful and concentrated climactic points in the whole sequence) transposes the comic and satirical effects to something grimly fantastic and grotesque and appalled.

My point is that we have been carried through a process of emotional clarification that is musically ordered, a music of feeling rather than a music of ideas, its dynamics determined by shifts in the intensity and lyric deployment of the successive passages. Attraction to life's most magnetic sources in body and spirit vies with fear of its consequences in the opening lines, and all the ensuing variations and modulations and transpositions open out and narrow down this central, active motive caught into the poem by the opening words, "April is the cruellest month. . . ." The two opposed sets of dramatic speech, one hysterically inward and the other savagely comic and externalized, of "A Game of Chess" provide yet another context for the same polar oppositions. Richness, then sheer need and distraction of spirit, then sardonic notes that pick up from those concealed in the serious Shakespearian parody at the start, then jazzy rhythms like those in Madame Sosostris's speech, then the chill paralysis of the sheer failure of feeling, and then the protracted complex mixture of low comedy, desperate grossness, and doomsday warning—these are, on the whole, the dominant succeed-

ing affects here. Still "mixing memory and desire" and the fear of pain
and of barrenness with both, the poem's genius lies in its prolificacy of
variations and of new tones that yet are controlled by the one original
emotional complex with which it began. The possibilities for more and
more variation, with a cumulative effect so long as redundancy is
avoided and the extent of the poem does not stifle the emotion, are not
inexhaustible although the limits of the power of any given sequence
are easier to discern than to characterize.

In any case, the extraordinary stylistic variations, and in particular
the varied lyric forms that interact with one another within this poetic
constellation and yet remain superbly independent, are what make this
poem the unique achievement it is. The possibilities of the initial
emotion are realized in a large number of directions within the same
magnetic field. The Bradleyan perspective serves the poet as a reminder
of the gulf between what we can actually know and the self-transcen-
dence to which we aspire. It makes any state of awareness keyed to
sharply defined insight (as opposed to passive immersion in experience)
in some sense an affirmation. States of ecstasy and horror can in this
sense be balanced on one side of the scale against sheer entropy. It can,
I think, be argued—though to demonstrate in detail would take many
pages—that *The Waste Land* despite some aberrations proceeds through
purer and purer intensities to extend and weigh the polarities with
which it begins, but that it need not necessarily have stopped where it
did. The surface rhetoric is in this sense an interference with the real
process of the poem.

Recovery of the earlier drafts shows us what some of the alternative
possibilities were. One needs to be open, not only to the deleted passages
as given us in the Valerie Eliot edition, but also to the possibilities they
represent. Whatever, for instance, one may think of the original first
section of "He Do the Police in Different Voices," it is important to
remember that its very presence would have changed the character of
the whole poem and that Eliot would probably have revised and
developed it differently in a final draft had he decided to keep it—as he
did, say, with the Tiresias passage whose first line originally read: "The
typist home at teatime, who begins. . . ." To start "The Burial of the
Dead" ("He Do the Police in Different Voices: Part I") with the long
account of a night out in Boston was a more daring idea than has been
recognized. It got the sequence off in low gear rather than at the highly
concentrated lyric pitch of the present opening. Thus the poem would
have lacked the advantage of an initial powerful center of reference
around which the rest of the sections would appear to be developed. On

the other hand, the idea of establishing a context of colloquialism and of commonplace urban life from the start had its own advantages:

> First we had a couple of feelers down at Tom's place,
> There was old Tom, boiled to the eyes, blind. . . .

The idiom becomes more specifically American a bit further on, and at the same time introduces the sexual theme without the romantic and emotional force it takes on a little later in the poem:

> —("I turned up an hour later down at Myrtle's place.
> What d'y'mean, she says, at two o'clock in the morning,
> I'm not in business here for guys like you;
> We've only had a raid last week. I've been warned twice. . . .

All this was difficult to manage, technically. Eliot had to get Boston Irish speech right, and also the normal hesitations and crude phrasing of most uncultivated conversation. Perhaps he meant to mingle the diction of college students with that of Myrtle and the local Irish-American speech. The cadences are abrupt though syncopated, and the allusions to current songs and Boston places are almost parochial. It is easy to dismiss what he does here, and yet the modulation toward a genuine poetry based on the speech of the streets is suggestive of a possibility for which the poetic situation was on the whole not yet ready. An atmosphere of casual and commercialized licentiousness is quickly established, as trivial and yet as cheating to the protagonist's real desires as the life of Marie. A certain ambience of confusion is established too. The love of music, theatre, erotic experience, and joy for its own sake, and the importance of magnanimity, are set forward as values despite the vulgarity of their manifestations. At the end of the passage the protagonist separates himself from the others—"I got out to see the sunrise, and walked home." It is the beginning of the journey among the levels of feeling and of moral condition that *The Waste Land* reports. And suddenly, in the next passage we are reading: "April is the cruellest month. . . ." The shift is a wrenching one, between extremes that mark out the opposite poles of consciousness in the poem. This was surely a potentially fruitful direction of the poem, one that might have informed it with a dimension of ordinary reality had the orientation been somewhat different.

In this context, the original beginning of "Death by Water," with its knowledgeable depiction of the life of sailors and the circumstances of serving on old sailing ships, also linked common experience with the larger motifs of the sequence. It is extremely interesting to see Eliot employing materials not unlike Masefield's while sustaining a highly formal precision of language in his own right and at the same time writing with a candor and a deliberate interrupting of his own formal tone that foreshadows the method of a poet like Charles Olson:

> The sailor, attentive to the chart and to the sheets,
> A concentrated will against the tempest and the tide,
> Retains, even ashore, in public bars and streets
> Something inhuman, clean, and dignified.
>
> Even the drunken ruffian who descends
> Illicit backstreet stairs, to reappear,
> For the derision of his sober friends,
> Staggering, or limping with a comic gonorrhea,
>
> From his trade with wind and sea and snow, as they
> Are, he is, with "much seen and much endured,"
> Foolish, impersonal, innocent or gay,
> Liking to be shaved, combed, scented, manicured. . . .

Elimination of this passage, and of the account of a ship's strange and sinister journey that follows, left only the brief "Phlebas the Phoenician" passage as Part IV. As with the deletion of the original opening lines of the poem, what was retained made for greater emphasis and clearer outlines. Yet if both passages had been retained, at the beginning of "The Burial of the Dead" and of "Death by Water," they would have constituted a continuing journey or quest pattern that would have prepared the reader for the Grail motif of "What the Thunder Said." The loose, halting rhythms of the deleted passage at the start were to be replaced by the firmer ones of the passage on the sailors' journey. Tragic proportion would thereby have been lent to the common life as we saw the sailors inexorably having to face their fate under a supernatural compulsion. The speaker's yearning toward that common life is now suggested only incidentally in a few lines of the poem. With retention of these two passages, it would have entered the poem's music more penetratingly whatever the effect on the total balance of the poem would have been.

Finally, had Eliot retained the Fresca passage at the head of "The Fire Sermon" and kept certain omitted lines about the "young man carbuncular" in the passage about the typist's seduction, a strong personal note of disgust and contempt would have altered the whole atmosphere of *The Waste Land*. His Swiftian revulsion at Fresca, the chic, vulgar female poetaster at her toilet and in society, violates the generous and emotionally open sensibility that seems to preside, otherwise, over most of the poem. A pettiness and meanness pervades the satire here, and the wit dissipates itself against a hardly formidable victim. That "Fresca slips softly to the needful stool" is hardly a powerful satirical point, and the following lines about her seem pathologically inflamed:

> This ended, to her steaming bath she moves,
> Her tresses fanned by little flutt'ring Loves;
> Odours, confected by the artful French,
> Disguise the good old hearty female stench.

These lines, and much of the rest that goes with them, give a bitchy flavor to Eliot's style that carries over to the scenes in "A Game of Chess" and to other scenes elsewhere in the poem. If retained, they would have destroyed the fine distancing generally maintained between the ultimate voice of the poem and the characters seen in closeup. Similarly, the contempt shown toward the young man and the typist in the original draft for their cultural pretensions obscures the essential bearing of the scene that depends in part on their viciousness being seen as ignorant and even innocent. And yet Eliot, had he kept these passages, would have committed himself to a much more confessional and vulnerable role in the structure of the poem. He would have had to set his own finicky and precious attitudes, and his abysmal feelings about female physicality, into the scale with other predominant motifs. These were possibilities of commitment toward which he went a fairly long way. In the era of Robert Lowell and Allen Ginsberg, he might well have gone the whole distance. Neither his nor Pound's taste was ready to be confident about doing so in 1922, and doubtless the best available reading public for poetry would not have been ready either. When he wrote, in the typist's seduction scene, that the young man

> Bestows one final patronising kiss,
> And gropes his way, finding the stairs unlit;
> And at the corner where the stable is,
> Delays only to urinate, and spit,

Pound crossed out the last two lines and wrote in the margin: "probably over the mark."

So *The Waste Land* is an open structure in two senses. The first sense is the one developed at the start of this essay, and has to do with the dynamics of the poem's movement as an extended lyric structure in sequence form. The structural principle resides not in ideas but in affects within a float of memories and associations in an ambiguous realm of consciousness, their direction determined by a driving emotional preoccupation. Intensities and modes of language define the structure; no story ends or argument completes itself here, but a momentary sense of balance provides a tentative sense of closure now and then.

The second kind of openness lies in the undeveloped potentialities suggested by excised portions of the earlier draft. We have not looked at all those passages, but have noted enough to show that certain colloquial modes of verse, and certain unattractive dimensions of personal feelings, were suppressed in the interests of an advanced poetics that was nevertheless not yet ready for them in the early 1920's. The feelings of the desired audience were a factor as well, as Pound's comment that I have just quoted would seem to indicate. A definite critical success was sought for *The Waste Land,* and that fact, and the two poets' stage of development at just that point, and Eliot's nervous condition all militated toward the inhibition of certain lines of exploration. Every poem is after all open in the sense that it could be developed further, it could be improved, if only the poet's energies and state of readiness were a trifle beyond their actual state. But *The Waste Land,* because of its place in the history of modern poetry and the peculiar history of its text, and because of its pioneering inward voyage by way of externalized images and other points of reference, is a particularly fascinating instance and problem.

Daniel R. Schwarz

The Failure of Meditation:
The Unity of Eliot's "Gerontion"

What has puzzled most readers of "Gerontion" is the apparently incoherent structure of the old man's monologue. But if it can be established that Eliot is dramatizing the process of unsuccessful meditation, the speaker's imprecision and incongruous combinations of sensual and spiritual images become explicable.[1] My contention is that "Gerontion" is about the title character's desperate attempt to place his life within an eschatological context and to achieve the humility and passionate commitment to Christ on which his salvation depends. By having Gerontion consciously quote Lancelot Andrewes and unconsciously parody a passage from Donne's *Second Anniversary,* Eliot implicitly juxtaposes Gerontion's monologue to the spiritual unity and concomitant rhetorical control of successful meditations within the

[1] If I were to select a paradigmatic statement of the view of the poem that I wish to refute, it would probably be the following comment from Mr. Grover Smith's excellent source study, *T. S. Eliot's Poetry & Plays: A Study in Source and Meaning* (Chicago: University of Chicago Press, 1956): "Because Gerontion, though primarily a symbol, is still dramatic enough to remain a person, the poem tends to split between the personality, which nevertheless is undefined, and the argument, which is not intimately enough related to the old man's feelings" (pp. 64-65).

In preparing this article, I have found two recent articles in *Sewanee Review* especially useful: John Crowe Ransom, "Gerontion," 74 (Spring, 1966), 389-414; and John Halverson, "Prufrock, Freud, and Others," 76 (Autumn, 1968), 571-588. I am also indebted to Louis L. Martz, *The Poetry of Meditation,* 2nd ed. (New York and New Haven: Yale University Press, 1962).

Reprinted in its original form by permission from The Bucknell Review, *19 (Spring, 1971), 55-76. Copyright* © Bucknell Review, *1970.*

contemptus mundi tradition.[2] Relying upon reason and logic to explain his inability to believe, while desperately groping for the faith on which salvation and apocalyptic vision depend, Gerontion's meditation poignantly dissolves into self-deprecation.

Because most of us are indebted to Professor Martz for showing us how the continental meditative treatises of the Counter Reformation influence the structure and content of seventeenth century religious poetry, it may be difficult for us to appreciate Eliot's immersion in the tradition of meditation. Yet only a man who felt a passionate epistemological empathy with this tradition could have written of Andrewes:

> It is only when we have saturated ourselves in his prose, followed the movement of his thought, that we find his examination of words terminating in the ecstasy of assent. Andrewes takes a word and derives the world from it; squeezing and squeezing the word until it yields a full juice of meaning which we should never have supposed any word to possess.[3]
>
> (p. 305)

Or,

> When Andrewes begins his sermon, from beginning to end you are sure that he is wholly in his subject, unaware of anything else, that his emotion grows as he penetrates more deeply into his subject, that he is finally "alone with the Alone," with the mystery which he is seeking to grasp more and more firmly.
>
> (p. 308)

By having Gerontion quote Andrewes as he recoils from the initial self-deprecation of the first verse paragraph, Eliot calls attention to the tradition of religious meditation in which his character is trying to participate. But the very qualities that Eliot praises in Andrewes' style—"ordonnance, or arrangement and structure, precision in the use of words, and relevant intensity"—are conspicuously lacking in Gerontion's monologue. In the same essay, Eliot goes on to compare Donne's sermons with Andrewes':

[2] The only critic that I know of to mention Eliot's use of *The Second Anniversary* is George Williamson in his *A Reader's Guide to T. S. Eliot,* 2nd ed. (New York: Noonday Press, 1966), who confines himself to noting that "the isolation of the imperatives to think ... calls to mind a comparable passage in Donne's *Second Anniversary*" (p. 110).

[3] Page numbers in parentheses refer to T. S. Eliot, *Selected Essays,* new ed. (New York: Harcourt, Brace & World, 1960).

Of the two men, it may be said that Andrewes is the more medieval, because he is the more pure, and because his bond was with the Church, with tradition. His intellect was satisfied by theology and his sensibility by prayer and liturgy. Donne is the more modern—if we are careful to take this word exactly without any implication of value, or any suggestion that we must have more sympathy with Donne than with Andrewes. Donne is much less mystic; he is primarily interested in man. He is much less traditional.   (p. 309)

It is hardly surprising that Eliot, himself, involved in a lifelong spiritual quest, used Donne's *Anniversaries* as a paradigm of the successful meditation if we recall Eliot's remark that Donne "belonged to that class of persons . . . who seek refuge in religion from the tumults of a strong emotional temperament which can find no complete satisfaction elsewhere" (p. 309).

I

At first Gerontion attempts to place himself in a sociological and historical context and to attribute his disillusionment and despair to a civilization which does not offer the opportunities for heroism or dignity. Gerontion sees himself not only as the victim but as a symbol of a civilization that he believes has deprived its best men of the opportunity to distinguish themselves in their actions. But the reader soon understands that Gerontion's negatives and circumlocutions thinly disguise his self-indulgent and narcissistic sensibility:

> I was neither at the hot gates
> Nor fought in the warm rain
> Nor knee deep in the salt marsh, heaving a cutlass,
> Bitten by flies, fought.[4]

If the opening two lines seem to indicate self-control and precision, this impression is quickly dispelled by the old man's savoring of the world of action that has passed him by. Rather than offering incisive self-analysis or a pointed indictment of his *Zeitgeist,* he fastidiously evokes the minor discomforts which he takes for the self-sacrifice that accompanies the heroic life. Although Gerontion begins the next sentence by teasing the reader into expecting a controlled analysis ("house" suggests both the physical body in which his soul dwells and

---

[4] *The Complete Poems and Plays* (New York: Harcourt, Brace & World, 1962).

the social and political world he inhabits), the syntactical precision is undercut by the vituperative substance:

> My house is a decayed house,
> And the jew squats on the window sill, the owner,
> Spawned in some estaminet of Antwerp,
> Blistered in Brussels, patched and peeled in London.

Devoting three lines to derogate the landlord with onomatopoeic verbs and participles—"squats," "spawned," "blistered," "patched," and "peeled"—is a gross example of the rhetoric of insult. In the next lines, Gerontion suggests that his era has witnessed the corruption of sexuality, symbolized by the sickly goat Capricorn, and family relations, represented by the infirmity of the anonymous woman who is reduced to a mere instrument for providing food and tea:

> The goat coughs at night in the field overhead;
> Rocks, moss, stonecrop, iron, merds.
> The woman keeps the kitchen, makes tea,
> Sneezes at evening, poking the peevish gutter.

But in view of his later self-consciousness about his declining capacity to feel ("I have lost my sight, smell, hearing, taste and touch"), it seems clear that the above statements are functions of Gerontion's psychic need to imagine himself as an archetype of a civilization that deprives men of a chance to distinguish themselves in action or to fulfill their emotional and spiritual needs. The concluding lines of the first verse paragraph indicate that his meditation is back at its self-pitying starting point.

The abrupt evocation of Andrewes' sermon on the Nativity stating the essence of Gerontion's dilemma represents a desperate attempt on Gerontion's part to leave what he realizes to be a bankrupt path of introspection:

> Signs are taken for wonders. "We would see a sign!"
> The word within a word, unable to speak a word,
> Swaddled with darkness. In the juvescence of the year
> Came Christ the tiger[5]

[5] The context for the sermon is taken from Matthew 12:39,40. As Professor Williamson points out, the sermon may be found in *Seventeen Sermons on the Nativity* (London, n.d.) with the passage that Eliot uses on pp. 200-201.

At the same time as he recalls Christ's rebuke to those Scribes and Pharisees who would wish for a demonstrable sign, he voices his own desperate hope for empirical evidence of grace. The "we" of the quotation enables him to distance his anxiety by generalizing it. That Gerontion cannot meditate upon the significance of Christ's Nativity and cannot translate the retelling of the event into insight is indicated simultaneously by the abrupt interruption of his sentence and by the implied pause before beginning again. The tiger not only suggests Blake's tiger, itself defined by antithesis to the Lamb, symbol of innocence, mercy, and humility, but also indicates that Christ is now a menacing image to Gerontion. Although Christ came at the appropriate time, "in the juvescence of the year," the response to Christ is inappropriate and degraded, coming as it does at the wrong time, "in depraved May," and accompanied by the icons of betrayal: dogwood and flowering judas. Rather than accepted in Christian humility and in the form of the traditional communion, Christ's presence is perverted by an assortment of aesthetes whose behavior is anticipated by the increasingly suspect series of words "to be eaten, to be divided, to be drunk among whispers." The description of those that take the Lord's supper gives these phrases a perverted and sordid import. Mr. Silvero, whose name hardly suggests an interest in spiritual values, apparently finds his spiritual satisfaction amongst his porcelain objects, and Hakagawa genuflects to his sensual Titians. While Madame de Tornquist perverts the communion by indulging in a séance, Fräulein von Kulp is conducting activities which seem to have more to do with the sexual than the religious realm.[6] Gerontion's bitterly perjorative epithet for these people, "Vacant shuttles weave the wind," ironically recalls the self-deprecatory phrase, "A dull head among windy spaces," and thus unintentionally forges a link between himself and the people he despises.

II

Before discussing how Eliot draws upon *The Second Anniversary*, perhaps I should make a few brief comments on *The Anniversaries*. Rather than viewing these remarkable religious poems as a personal statement of Donne's, I believe that Donne is dramatizing the process of discovering spiritual certainties amidst excruciating and agonizing

[6] Ransom reminds us that Fräulein von Kulp's name suggests *culpa,* guilt. See Ransom, [op. cit.] p.402.

doubts that his *Zeitgeist* presented to him. Certainly Donne, just as Eliot, draws upon his own epistemological experience, but the very fact that he chooses to meditate upon the significance of the death of a young girl that he barely knew indicates that he is concerned with understanding the meaning of death rather than with presenting an outpouring of private grief. In 1920 Eliot would have approved of Donne's division between the man who suffers and the mind that creates, of his "continual surrender of himself as he is at the moment to something which is more valuable" (p. 7). Indeed, Donne's persona sets out to perform a vatic role, to sing Elizabeth Drury's praises, because "none/Offers to tell us who'it is that's gone" (I.42).[7] It soon becomes apparent that the speaker does not mean to discuss her specific virtues, or even her significance as the platonic symbol of goodness on earth, but the relationship of this life to the next and the possibilities of salvation for those remaining on earth. The subject of the poem, then, is at once anonymous since the deceased is barely mentioned except in terms of what she symbolizes, and highly personalized, because the significance of her death to the speaker is the poem's subject. By coming to understand the implications of the death of a young girl, the speaker discovers an inclusive system of spiritual values.

Like the persona of *The Anniversaries,* Gerontion contemplates the problem of belief at a time when he feels an inadequacy in his faith. While Elizabeth Drury's death makes Donne's speaker think of the world as "fragmentary rubbidge," Gerontion's dissatisfaction with his *own* plight leads him to indict the world. While in *The Anniversaries* the speaker moves from despair to faith and finally to a point where he imagines himself having a vision of God, in "Gerontion" the speaker cannot reconcile himself to death because he cannot meditate effectively.[8] Gerontion intellectually knows that he lacks the faith on which salvation depends, but knowledge of his plight is not enough.

That Gerontion meditates upon history in the passage whose structure echoes Donne is fraught with ironic implication. In the passage that Eliot has his speaker parody, Donne's persona meditates upon the significance of Elizabeth Drury in an intense dialogue between self and soul:

[7] *John Donne: The Anniversaries*, ed. Frank Manley (Baltimore: Johns Hopkins, 1963).

[8] For a more detailed discussion of Donne's *Anniversaries*, see my "The Failure of Meditation: The Unity of Eliot's 'Gerontion,' " *Bucknell Review*, 19 (1971), 55-76.

> Thinke then, My soule, that death is but a Groome,
> Which brings a Taper to the outward roome,
> Whence thou spiest first a little glimmering light,
> And after brings it nearer to thy sight:
> For such approaches doth Heaven make in death.   (II.85-89)

> Thinke in how poore a prison thou didst lie
> After enabled but to sucke, and crie. . . .
> But thinke that Death hath now enfranchis'd thee,
> Thou hast thy'expansion now and libertee; . . .
>   (II.173-174; 179-180)

The pronoun "she," which in "Geronion" denotes the secular abstraction "history" and which is the object of sexual innuendoes, refers in *The Anniversaries* to Elizabeth Drury, who becomes a symbol of the possibility of achieving the promise of salvation that is the goal of Donne's persona's spiritual quest. Ironically and poignantly Geronion returns to the temporal and geographical framework of his opening remarks. After demonstrating that he understands how Christ's meaning has been made a sham by the aesthetes and self-conceived spiritualists, he displays his own spiritual hollowness by meditating upon history. Rather than meditate on the significance of the Christian mystery, such as the inexplicable death of a young girl or the meaning of some of Christ's words to the Scribes and Pharisees, Geronion turns to the very discipline that provides a logical explanation for his present plight. He would try to explain his inadequacy by placing himself in the context of a concatenation of events over which he has no control:

> Think now
> History has many cunning passages, contrived corridors
> And issues, deceives with whispering ambitions,
> Guides us by vanities. Think now
> She gives when our attention is distracted
> And what she gives, gives with such supple confusions
> That the giving famishes the craving. Gives too late
> What's not believed in, or if still believed,
> In memory only, reconsidered passion. Gives too soon
> Into weak hands, what's thought can be dispensed with
> Till the refusal propagates a fear. Think
> Neither fear nor courage saves us. Unnatural vices
> Are fathered by our heroism. Virtues
> Are forced upon us by our impudent crimes.

But in *The Second Anniversary,* which is the model of successful meditation against which Eliot is intentionally juxtaposing Gerontion's ineffectual attempts at meditation, Donne's persona counsels his soul to disregard the threat of death and the concerns of this world.

Gerontion's conception of history is unilinear and dialectic; it is the accumulation of causes that explain his *personal* dilemma at a certain spatial-temporal locus. For Gerontion history is merely a concatenation of events tested by empirical knowledge and formulated into causes; he eschews the possibility that historical events may become transformed into eternal moments. The speaker in "East Coker" (1940)—virtually inseparable from the poet himself—provides an illuminating critique of Gerontion's dialogue with history. In "East Coker," the speaker not only rejects empirical knowledge, but even more significantly, his passionate dialogue between self and soul suggests the proper way to achieve salvation:

> I said to my soul, be still, and let the dark come upon you
> Which shall be the darkness of God. . . .
>
> I said to my soul, be still, and wait without hope
> For hope would be hope for the wrong thing; wait without love
> For love would be love of the wrong thing; there is yet faith
> But the faith and the love and the hope are all in the waiting.
>
> ("East Coker," III)

We should realize that Gerontion's imperatives are not directed to his soul but to *himself.* His inability to perceive the soul as a separate entity is itself symptomatic of a lack of grace. He precedes his meditation with the despairing question, "After such knowledge, what forgiveness?" a question that follows his reiteration that he is an "old man . . . under a windy knob." Obviously, despite his having evoked Christ and quoted Andrewes and his insight that his contemporaries have perverted the meaning of the communion, his continual lapses into self-pity and ennui are indicative of his failure to believe passionately. In *The Anniversaries,* the speaker imagines himself performing a vatic role for all who have a soul, while Gerontion seeks the *comfort* of generalizing his plight to include his generation. If history is at fault and we are all the inevitable effects of causes beyond our control, then it follows that Gerontion's plight is not personal but representative and that he can speak of "us" and "our." The pathetic need to generalize the spiritual drought, to move from the first person singular to the first person plural, is in stark contrast to the intense introspective dialogue of *The Second Anniversary*, which increasingly proceeds as if the immediate and intuitive relationship with God were the only reality and that nothing else could possibly affect this relationship.

III

That Gerontion recognizes the futility of his meditation on history is indicated by his awareness that his tears are not the result of penitence: "These tears are shaken from the wrath-bearing tree." He has emphasized the necessity for moisture to allay his spiritual drought. But these are tears resulting from indignation and anger with a world that has made him what he is. The "wrath-bearing tree" recalls Blake's poem, "A Poison Tree," where the tree of wrath is watered by fears and sunned by "soft deceitful wiles" until it becomes capable of deadly evil. Gerontion is operating within the post-Enlightenment Blakean cosmos without his being consciously aware of it. The very next words after "wrath-bearing tree" are "the tiger"; the Blakean tiger of "The Tyger" and *The Marriage of Heaven and Hell* is antithetical to the meaning of the Lamb and suggests punishment for, rather than forgiveness of, sins. Gerontion's allusions emphasize his distance from the spirit of Bishop Andrewes and Donne's persona. It is useful to recall Eliot's condescending remarks about Blake's system of beliefs, remarks that were made at about the same time that "Gerontion" was first published:

> We have the same respect for Blake's philosophy . . . that we have for an ingenious piece of home-made furniture: we admire the man who has put it together out of the odds and ends about the house. England has produced a fair number of these resourceful Robinson Crusoes; but we are not really so remote from the Continent, or from our own past, as to be deprived of the advantages of culture if we wish them.

> And about Blake's supernatural territories, as about the supposed ideas that dwell there, we cannot help commenting on a certain meanness of culture. . . . What his genius required, and what it sadly lacked, was a framework of accepted and traditional ideas which would have prevented him from indulging in a philosophy of his own. . . .   (p. 279)[9]

[9] The Blake essay, anthologized in the *Selected Essays* as "William Blake," appeared as a review in 1920, the year that "Gerontion" was first published in the volume *Ara Vos Prec.*

The statement of renewal, "The tiger springs in the new year. Us he devours." is really an expression of hope which loses its significance in the face of Gerontion's failure to meditate on the meaning of this posited resurrection. Christ's rebirth, properly understood, is the end of the Tiger of Wrath and the Old Dispensation. But the very word "devours" implies that for him Christ is a threat that terrifies because his notion of Christ is as a punishing Tiger of Wrath.

The sexual innuendoes with which Gerontion discusses history become more and more obtrusive and finally culminate with the crude pun on "stiffening":

> Think at last
> We have not reached conclusion, when I
> Stiffen in a rented house.

The passage echoing the most intense and passionate moments of *The Second Anniversary* has degenerated into an elegy for an old man's sexual prowess. As if to show Gerontion's inherent crudeness, Eliot has his character speak in *double entendres*. History is conceived of as a temptress who "deceives with whispering ambitions,/ Guides us by vanities." More explicitly, this Cleopatra Figure "gives with such supple confusions/ That the giving famishes the craving." At one level he is rebuking history for using her "cunning passages" to deceive men into committing deeds in spite of themselves. That Gerontion speaks in sexual terms places him within the crude *Zeitgeist* that he would separate himself from; it also bathetically undercuts the very concept that Gerontion takes seriously.

The movement of the meditative passage containing the imperative "think" is away from the discovery of faith and towards self-pity. It is ironic that the last imperative "think" alludes to the devils in Dante's inferno that run backwards. For Gerontion has become another of those devils that run backwards, since his rhetoric moves further and further from the Word and its contingent mysteries and towards the secular and sensual concerns that continue to intrude upon his meditative efforts. Finally abandoning the specific meditative pattern that echoes Donne, Gerontion attempts to vindicate himself to God with the pathetic plea, "I would meet you upon this honestly." But this new approach to Christ is yet another way of avoiding prayer and repentence, for now he would speak to Christ logically and coherently, would attempt again to explain and extenuate his plight. The reason, he explains, that he has lost his passion is that his senses have failed him:

I that was near your heart was removed therefrom
To lose beauty in terror, terror in inquisition.
I have lost my passion: why should I need to keep it
Since what is kept must be adulterated?
I have lost my sight, smell, hearing, taste and touch:
How should I use them for your closer contact?

Yet I think Eliot wishes us to see that Gerontion's optics are still wrong. Sense experience is not the way to discover the essential faith for salvation. The decline of the senses, a natural result of old age, is not the cause of Gerontion's failure to achieve the "closer contact" that he knows is essential. The example of Hakagawa, Mr. Silvero, and the rest of the participants in the ineffectual communion should have made clear to Gerontion that it is not his atrophied senses that prevent him from finding the faith with which to experience Christ. In the next sentence when he borrows images from the material world to describe his plight, he ironically locates himself within the *Zeitgeist* that he had taken pains to reject in the first and third verse paragraphs:

These with a thousand small deliberations
Protract the profit of their chilled delirium,
Excite the membrane, when the sense has cooled,
With pungent sauces, multiply variety
In a wilderness of mirrors.

Now he realizes that his meditation is no more than a "thousand small deliberations" providing intellectual and emotional titillation, and that he is caught in a psychic house of mirrors from which there is no escape.

IV

Gerontion finds it increasingly difficult to follow through on his ideas or even to make syntactical sense. His meditation moves in the direction of fragmentation and dubiety. At an obvious level, Gerontion partakes of the parasitic nature of the weevil and the spider that he inquires about:

What will the spider do,
Suspend its operation, will the weevil
Delay?

Like the spider and the weevil, Gerontion himself is caught up in the process of mutability and mortality which he lacks the faith to transcend. Thoughts of mortality evoke the vision of bodies, presumably belonging to the decadent spatial-temporal locus that he seeks to escape, "whirled/Beyond the circuit of the shuddering Bear/In fractured atoms." His entire epistemology at this point is non-Christian, indicative of the failure of his attempts to find faith. His reference to the Big Dipper, "the shuddering Bear," recalls his earlier reference to the lecherous Capricorn. And he believes that the dead will become mere particles of matter rather than taking their place as souls within a Christian framework containing heaven, hell, and limbo.

Ironically, Gerontion has earned his right to be identified with those passive creatures who are the helpless victims of natural process. As he is caught up in the process of history because he lacks the faith to escape, the gull is caught in the wind:

> Gull against the wind, in the windy straits
> Of Belle Isle, or running on the Horn,
> White feathers in the snow, the Gulf claims,
> And an old man driven by the Trades
> To a sleepy corner.

The image of the gull swept in spite of itself to Belle Isle (perhaps a parody of Ulysses' destination of the "happy Isles," a destination that Tennyson's heroic figure consciously reaches for) or the Gulf (perhaps, as Ransom suggests, the Abyss in the bottom of the world) again places Gerontion's cosmology in a non-Christian framework. Even the references to weather and to the literal geography, such as Cape Horn and the Gulf of Mexico, show how far he has strayed from his original quest of coming to terms with death and preparing his soul for salvation. Ironically, the speaker is a gull in the traditional sense, a foolish victim of his own winds, and he will die, like the bird, isolated and without consequence. In this sentence, "an old man driven by the Trades" is in virtual apposition to the gull, and the phrase "White feathers in the snow" becomes almost a metonymy for the speaker who conflates his vision of the gull's death with that of his own. The general term, "an old man," thinly disguises Gerontion's admission that he is equal to the gull in his impotence to resist a meaningless death.[10]

[10] What Reuben Brower has said about the importance of allusion in Dryden and Pope is equally applicable to Eliot: "Allusion, especially as ironic contexts, is a resource equivalent to symbolic metaphor and elaborate imagery in other

In contrast to the spiritual ecstasy which Donne's speaker attains in his meditation, Gerontion lapses into ineffectual despair at the failure of his attempts to reach Christ and finally drifts into self-pitying silence. The final crystallizing image of the "old man" driven into a corner from which there is no escape is underlined by the final dreary refrain:

> Tenants of the house,
> Thoughts of a dry brain in a dry season.

These lines bring together two image patterns which allude persistently to Donne's poem. Gerontion's emphasis on dryness and his emphasis on living in a "decayed house" take on renewed significance if we recall *The Anniversaries.* The persona of Donne's poem advises his soul to continually thirst for the Eucharist:

> Thirst for that time, O my insatiate soule,
> And serve thy thirst, with God's safe-sealing Bowle.
> Bee thirsty still, and drinke still till thou goe;
> 'Tis th' onely Health, to be Hydropique so.   (II. 45-58)

---

poets." (*Alexander Pope: The Poetry of Allusion* [Oxford, England: The Clarendon Press, 1959], p. viii). The complexity of the allusive technique in "Gerontion" extends to the epigraph taken from the Duke's advice to Claudio in *Measure for Measure* to "be absolute for death." The Duke's secular version of the *contemptus mundi* tradition only momentarily provides Claudio with an epistemology with which to face death. Gerontion's attempt for positional assurance is implicitly contrasted with the Duke's avowal that death is a trifle. But Gerontion resembles Claudio, whose original acceptance of the Duke's advice gives way to doubt and fear and whose vision of death anticipates Gerontion's images of dead bodies whirled through space:

> Ay, but to die, and go we know not where,
> To lie in cold obstruction and to rot
> This sensible warm motion to become
> A kneaded clod; and the delightful spirit
> To bathe in fiery floods, or to reside
> In thrilling region of thick-ribbèd ice,
> To be imprisoned in the viewless winds
> And blown with restless violence round about
> The pendent world; . . .   (*Measure for Measure*, ed. R. C. Bald
> [Baltimore: Penguin, 1956] III.i.118-126)

Not only is Gerontion's fear of continual physical atrophy that will culminate in complete stasis anticipated in the first lines; also suggested by Claudio's terror are the specifics of Gerontion's vision. Claudio's image of the dead's domain as a "thrilling region of thick-ribbèd ice" is evoked by Gerontion's depicting the feathers of the gull—with the bitterly self-conscious meaning of fool and dupe—strewn on the snow.

Gerontion recognizes the need for life-giving water, but concludes significantly as "a dry brain in a dry season," knowing he is further from the "warm rain" than ever. In both Eliot and Donne, the house becomes a metaphor for both the body and the physical world. Donne's speaker welcomes death as a release because man is poorly "housed" in his "living Tombe":

> Shee, shee, thus richly and largely hous'd, is gone:
> And chides us slow-pac'd snailes who crawle upon
> Our prison's prison, earth, nor thinke us well,
> Longer, then whil'st wee bear our' brittle shell.
> But 'twere but little to have chang'd our roome,
> If, as we were in this our living Tombe
> Oppress'd with ignorance, wee still were so.   (II. 247-253)

Gerontion does not realize the irrelevance of his complaints about his decayed house, an image which expands to imply contemporary Europe and contracts to imply his physical body. Were he able to believe passionately in Christ as the Lamp of mercy and salvation, the declining physical condition of his body and the decaying civilization of Europe would not be of any importance.

V

For Eliot, poetry is a creative art, "a way of putting it" for his audience, but poetry is also the means of working out his most compelling personal dilemmas. While it can be said that every poem contains part of the poet, it is especially true of Eliot. As Professor Austin has recently shown, "Eliot does not deny that the work of any poet may express personality but contends that the work of a mature poet possesses 'a greater expression of personality' and that this expression increases esthetic value."[11] Despite his public language and allusions, Eliot's is a far more private poetry than is generally realized, a private poetry in the way that Herbert's poetry is private, dramatizing a personal religious quest involving crises of conscience and agonies of doubt. Eliot isolates tendencies within himself and creates a distinct personality from attitudes and emotions which he recognizes as part of his own personality. Eliot wrote that a "dramatic poet cannot create characters of the greatest intensity of life unless his personages, in their

[11] Allen Austin, "T. S. Eliot's Theory of Personal Expression," *PMLA*, 81 (June, 1966), 305.

reciprocal action and behavior in their story, are somehow dramatizing, but in no obvious form, an action or struggle for harmony in the soul of the poet" (pp. 172-173).[12] Beginning with Prufrock's insistence on asking cosmic questions, Eliot is increasingly concerned with the problem of religious belief in a secular age when, as he remarks in the Andrewes' essay, "all dogma is in doubt except the dogmas of science of which we have read in newspapers, when the language of theology itself, under the influence of an undisciplined mysticism of popular philosophy, tends to become a language of tergiversation" (p. 305). In Eliot's major works, there is a progressive narrowing of distance between speaker and poet until in the *Four Quartets* the persona and the poet are well-nigh indistinguishable. Perhaps dramatizing the unsuccessful struggle for spiritual conviction in "Gerontion" and "The Love Song of J. Alfred Prufrock" was part of Eliot's own religious quest and helped to prepare his spiritual and poetic energies for the great religious poetry of *Ash-Wednesday* and the *Four Quartets*.

[12] See Eliot's "The Three Voices of Poetry," *On Poetry and Poets*, Noonday Press ed. (New York: Noonday, 1961), pp. 96-112.

Leonard Unger

"*The Hollow Men*" *and* Ash-Wednesday

Both "The Hollow Men" and *Ash-Wednesday* began as short individual poems published independently in periodicals, and the pieces were later fitted together and other sections added to make the completed longer poems. This piecemeal mode of composition is emphasized by the fact that some of the short poems written during the same period and having similar themes, style, and imagery are excluded from "The Hollow Men" and in the collected editions preserved among the *Minor Poems*. There is a nice implication here—that "minor" pieces, when assembled under an inclusive title and according to some thematic and cumulative principle, produce a "major" and more formidable whole. The relationship between whole and parts is again suggested by the *Ariel Poems*, first published between 1927 and 1930 (except for "The Cultivation of Christmas Trees," 1954), the same period during which *Ash-Wednesday* was taking shape. The earlier *Ariel Poems* are closely related in structure, style, and meaning to those poems which eventually became sections of *Ash-Wednesday*. It is conceivable that some of the *Ariel Poems* might have been built into larger wholes and the earliest sections of *Ash-Wednesday* left as separate poems. As it is, the *Ariel Poems* make a kind of series of appendixes to *Ash-Wednesday*.

Turning from the external to the internal, we find in "The Hollow Men" and *Ash-Wednesday* the same features already noted in earlier

From Leonard Unger, T. S. Eliot: Moments and Patterns, *University of Minnesota Press, Minneapolis,* ©*1956, 1961, 1966 by the University of Minnesota.*

work. In "The Hollow Men" the themes of the fragmentary and the inarticulate are represented by both the form and the content of the statements. Throughout the poem the themes are symbolized by a wealth of images, and especially notable are "broken glass," "broken column," "broken stone," and "broken jaw." At the opening of the poem the voices of the hollow men "Are quiet and meaningless," and toward the end their speech is broken into stammered fragments of the Lord's Prayer. The first and last passages of the final section are inane and sinister parodies of a children's game song. Similar elements are present in *Ash-Wednesday*. The poem begins with the translated quotation from Cavalcanti, and this is immediately broken into fragments, thus suggesting, among other things, the speaker's struggle to find expression:

> Because I do not hope to turn again
> Because I do not hope
> Because I do not hope to turn . . .

Exactly the same passage, but with "Because" changed to "Although," opens the final section of the poem. Section II is centrally concerned with fragmentation as symbolized by the scattered bones which sing, "We are glad to be scattered, we did little good to each other." As for the problem of articulation, it is the "unspoken word" which is the central concern of section V:

> Where shall the word be found, where will the word
> Resound? Not here, there is not enough silence
> Not on the sea or on the islands, not
> On the mainland, in the desert or the rain land . . .

The final words of the poem are "Suffer me not to be separated/ And let my cry come unto Thee." These statements are fragments quoted from Catholic ritual—and they clearly convey both of the familiar and related themes: isolation (which is also fragmentation) and spiritual communion (which is also articulation).

In the collected editions of Eliot's poetry, placed between *Ariel Poems* and *Minor Poems*, there is a section called "Unfinished Poems." This is comprised of *Sweeney Agonistes* and "Coriolan." The two parts of *Sweeney Agonistes* are "Fragment of a Prologue" and "Fragment of an Agon," and they first appeared in 1926 and 1927 respectively. Arranged together, they are described by Eliot in a subtitle as "Fragments of an Aristophanic Melodrama." But *Sweeney Agonistes* is not actually an "unfinished" work. Each part and the two parts together are deliberate ironical parodies of surviving fragments of classical texts, and thus the fragmentariness is a justifiable aspect of the finished product. The device of parodying (classical) fragments provided Eliot with an opportunity for experimental exercises in the use of dramatic verse and thus also in the use of rhythms borrowed from the conventions of the music hall and of colloquial speech. Another aspect of the fragmentariness is the deliberate continuity with, or reiteration of, elements from his earlier work—meaning, of course, that Sweeney had first appeared in the quatrains of *Poems* (1920) and then again briefly in *The Waste Land.* In the satirically trite and empty speech which makes up so much of the dialogue in these pieces, the subject of articulation, of communication, is plainly implicit, and it is finally explicit in the lines spoken by Sweeney toward the end of the second "Fragment":

> I gotta use words when I talk to you
> But if you understand or if you dont
> That's nothing to me and nothing to you . . .

The fragmentariness of *Sweeney Agonistes* is a structural device, but also, as in earlier works, it is related to subject and meaning. "Coriolan," on the other hand, is appropriately described as "unfinished." Its two sections, "Triumphal March" and "Difficulties of a Statesman," appeared respectively in 1931 and 1932. The work was apparently motivated by the political pressures of the time. Eliot's description of "Coriolan" as unfinished is meaningful in a number of ways. It obviously signifies that a suite of sections constituting a larger and self-contained work was intended. Eliot clearly abandoned the project at an early date, for in *Collected Poems 1909-1935* the work is already classified as unfinished. And "Coriolan" does have a quality of incompleteness in greater measure than is characteristic of Eliot's work. There is, for example, more "completeness," more clarity of effect, a more decided achievement of tone, in any section of *The Waste Land* or "The Hollow Men" or *Ash-Wednesday.* Perhaps Eliot was aware of this measure of failure in deciding to abandon the project and then to classify it as unfinished. It was, in fact, uncharacteristic of Eliot to have projected a poem on so large a scale, and the failure of the project is therefore significant. When questioned by an interviewer, Eliot clearly acknowledged what was otherwise implicit in his practice. To the

question whether *Ash-Wednesday* had begun as separate poems, he
answered: "Yes, like "The Hollow Men," it originated out of separate
poems. . . . Then gradually I came to see it as a sequence. That's one
way in which my mind does seem to have worked throughout the years
poetically—doing things separately and then seeing the possibility of
fusing them together, altering them, and making a kind of whole of
them."

A *kind* of whole—that is an apt and significant description. That
kind of whole is nowhere more obvious than in what appears to be
Eliot's final major performance in nondramatic verse, the *Four Quartets*. He has informed us that the first of these, "Burnt Norton," grew
out of passages deleted from his play *Murder in the Cathedral.* The
Four Quartets was hardly conceived as "a kind of whole" at the time of
the composition of "Burnt Norton." That poem, eventually to be the
first Quartet, appeared in 1935, and the next Quartet, "East Coker,"
not until 1940. Thus the *Four Quartets* had an unpremeditated beginning in the salvaging of fragments removed from the play. "Burnt
Norton" itself becomes a "kind of fragment" in retrospect from the
other Quartets. In the years immediately following its appearance it
received relatively little attention, while the *Four Quartets* was soon,
and then often, praised as Eliot's supreme achievement. By itself,
"Burnt Norton" revealed themes and elements of structure familiar
enough against the background of earlier work. Like *The Waste Land*, it
is divided into five sections. It has affinities of meaning and style with
Ash-Wednesday and *Murder in the Cathedral,* and also with the play
The Family Reunion, which came later (1939). But in serving as the
model for the other three quartets, it derived a clarity of structure and
patterning of themes which could not otherwise be claimed for it. To
extend the musical metaphor of the inclusive title, it is the variations
which locate and define the theme. And it is that title which announces
most succinctly the quasi-wholeness and the quasi-fragmentariness
which are characteristic of Eliot's work. The title *Four Quartets* allows
for the separate unity of each of the Quartets, and at the same time
makes each a part of the larger whole.

While this ambivalence of parts and wholes is a structural con-
venience of which Eliot had always availed himself, it operates with
special purpose in *Four Quartets.* A central subject of the work is the
relation of the individual consciousness and identity to the passage of
time—and time is meaningful in the work not only as a consideration
and a grounds of discourse, but also in respect to the history of the

composition of *Four Quartets,* to its having been written over a period of time. During this period of time there were changes in the poet's attitudes. According to "Burnt Norton," "To be conscious is not to be in time." Escape from time into consciousness is achieved in the transcendent ecstasy symbolized by "the moment in the rose-garden," so that all other time, unless it is a means to this end, is meaningless:

> Ridiculous the waste sad time
> Stretching before and after.

The later Quartets, on the other hand, are less subjective and are increasingly concerned with reconciling the temporal and the timeless—as toward the end of "The Dry Salvages":

> . . . And right action is freedom
> From past and future also.
> For most of us, this is the aim
> Never here to be realised;
> Who are only undefeated
> Because we have gone on trying . . .

Four Quartets is (or are) essentially meditative and reflective poetry, but the mode of composition over a period of time, the fresh attack in each Quartet on the same themes, the willingness to acknowledge and define changes in attitude—these give a dramatic quality to the reflections. The changes wrought by time are thus not only a general subject of the work, they are a particularized and dramatized meaning, and in being such they are also a lineament of the form. The poet's awareness of this fact is among the reflections he makes in the poetry. In "East Coker" there is the plaintive observation that "every attempt/ Is a wholly new start," and in "The Dry Salvages" the problem is expressed again, this time as a broad, less subjectively personal preoccupation:

> . . . time is no healer: the patient is no longer here.
> . . . .
> You are not the same people who left that station
> Or who will arrive at any terminus . . .

Each of the Quartets and then all of them together have a greater conventional unity than Eliot's previous nondramatic poetry. Whereas so much of the earlier work is a direct representation of the fragmentariness of experience, *Four Quartets* is a deliberate and sustained discourse on that subject, and it ends with a serene vision of that wholeness which lies beyond the reach of time:

> And all shall be well and
> All manner of thing shall be well
> When the tongues of flames are in-folded
> Into the crowned knot of fire
> And the fire and the rose are one.

As in earlier work, the problem of articulation is among the interrelated themes of *Four Quartets*. In *Ash-Wednesday* blame was placed upon the external world for this problem:

> . . . there is not enough silence
> .   .   .   .
> The right time and the right place are not here . . .

The same complaint is made in the early Quartets, as in the final section of "Burnt Norton":

> . . . Words strain,
> Crack and sometimes break, under the burden,
> Under the tension, slip, slide, perish,
> Decay with imprecision, will not stay in place,
> Will not stay still. Shrieking voices
> Scolding, mocking, or merely chattering,
> Always assail them.

In "East Coker" the poet complains of "the intolerable wrestle/ With words and meanings." If it is impossible to say just what he means, this is because his meanings have changed with the passage of time,

> Because one has only learnt to get the better of words
> For the thing one no longer has to say, or the way in which
> One is no longer disposed to say it.

Blame is still put upon the external world, for the struggle must be made, he says,

> . . . now, under conditions
> That seem unpropitious.

In the final Quartet, "Little Gidding," there is greater candor, greater
objectivity, an acknowledgment of his own achievement, but still a note
of alienation, as the poet sees his work (so long a dominant and
determining influence) recede with the passage of time into the perspective of literary history:

> . . . Last season's fruit is eaten
> And the fullfed beast shall kick the empty pail.
> For last year's words belong to last year's language
> And next year's words await another voice.

In the last section of "Little Gidding" there is a final statement on the
subject, a statement which combines a celebration of the possible with
an acceptance of the inevitable.

> . . . And every phrase
> And sentence that is right (where every word is at home,
> Taking its place to support the others,
> The word neither diffident nor ostentatious,
> An easy commerce of the old and the new,
> The common word exact without vulgarity,
> The formal word precise but not pedantic,
> The complete consort dancing together)
> Every phrase and every sentence is an end and a beginning,
> Every poem an epitaph.

William T. Moynihan

Character and Action in Four Quartets

Although Eliot's *Four Quartets* is essentially a dramatic meditation, it is more often discussed as though it were a didactic poem.[1] Perhaps this is an inevitable result of the poem's complexities—its orchestrated themes, its references and allusions, and its mixture of lyric and prosaic passages. But, regardless of the reason for this approach, the critical emphasis has been on what the speaker says rather than on who he is and how his character orders his reflections. What now needs to be emphasized is that the *Quartets* is not primarily a poem of ideas, but a poem about the experience of ideas. Or, to apply one of Eliot's own distinctions, it does not so much set forth a belief as it tells us how a believer feels.

If we were not concerned with the quality of the consciousness of the speaker, or with the emotional impact of the lyric and dramatic contexts of his meditation, we could reduce the themes in the *Four Quartets* to any number of perennial religious truisms—"love," "have

[1] Most critics do not classify the *Four Quartets*. The majority of the critics treat it as a didactic poem; a few even seem to feel Eliot intended to write *An Essay on Man*. Hugh Kenner puts forth the majority position of critics when he writes: "To devise a measure is to devise a voice, and the appropriate range of expressive content the Voice implies. Of this Voice we may remark first of all its selflessness; it is old Possum's last disappearing-trick. No persona, Prufrock, Gerontion, Tiresias or the Magus, is any longer needed." (*The Invisible Poet*, New York, 1959, p. 293). Eliot did not devise his musical format in the *Quartets* in order to make his didacticism more palatable. The different poetic styles and intensities would seem rather to represent the fluctuations of the speaker's mind as he wrestles with grasping the relationship between human time and God's time—or perhaps more accurately—God's timelessness.

Reprinted by permission from Mosaic, *6 (Fall, 1972), 203-228. Copyright © 1972 by The Editors,* Mosaic, *The University of Manitoba Press.*

faith," "be humble," or, to use the triad Eliot himself made famous, "give, sympathize, control." Perhaps a rudimentary but essential act of criticism would be to read in rapid succession Eliot's *The Choruses from the Rock* and the *Quartets*. There are few, if any, ideas in the *Quartets* which are not in the *Choruses*. But the *Choruses* give no sense of a speaker in the act of thinking, a man trying—in Stevens' phrase—to find "what will suffice." The *Quartets* presents such a man; the *Choruses* presents a preacher expounding. The *Quartets* presents both the speaker in the act of recalling his experience of life and the emotional effect of that recalling.

Thus, although the *Quartets* clearly articulates the effects of a religious view of the world on a man's mind and action, it does not have as its main purpose to present a philosophy of life as a truly didactic poem would—Pope's *Essay on Man* or Johnson's *The Vanity of Human Wishes*. In the *Quartets* the speaker's emotional involvement in his reflections and the reader's assumed involvements are of prime importance. And while Eliot was obviously not as intent as Browning would have been to give his speaker a clearly autonomous dramatic existence, he nevertheless gives him a personality distinctly appropriate to his reflections.

Everything in the poem aims at miming the emotional quality of the speaker's thought. Even the poetic and prosaic alternations—the perfect formal lyrics and the passages of poetic prose—are designed to reveal the feelings of the speaker. Eliot himself wrote "passages of greater and less intensity . . . give a rhythm of fluctuating emotion."[2] But the style serves only the purpose of a tonal background, and does not give a very precise idea of who the speaker is. In order to grasp that, we must try to determine the action of the poem and what motivates this action, observe the specific emotional qualities of the speaker's language, place this speaker among similar speakers in Eliot's work, and consider the speaker's relationship with this audience. Thus, and in greater detail, we will be ready to answer the question concerning how the speaker's character is related to the ordering of his thought—an ordering which we will find to be ritualistic.

Simply stated, the action of the *Quartets* presents a limited, uncertain human intelligence trying to grasp the meaning of the Divine Logos. Eliot's epigraphs from Herakleitos suggest both the problem of any human mind coming into union with divine wisdom, and a possible solution. The problem is that every individual has his own concept of

---

[2] T. S. Eliot, *The Music of Poetry* (Glasgow, 1928), pp. 24-25.

wisdom—in the poem Eliot provides the best example of this when dealing with human views of time implicitly compared with God's timelessness. The solution is implied in "The way up and the way down are the same," and lies in the concept of relatedness. Just as the elements—earth, air, fire and water—are chemically related to one another, so God's world, God's time, God's logos connects with man. And any small perception of God's wisdom may allow man to follow the chain of spiritual connections towards God's timelessness. What for the Greeks was a downward movement from fire to earth thus becomes in Eliot an upward movement from intimations of immortality in a rose garden to the fire of "Little Gidding."

There seems an assumption on the part of some readers that because Eliot, as author, knows the end of his speaker's meditation before he begins, and because his speaker's faith remains constant, there can be little or no dramatic tension in the poem. But the speaker of the poem is a fictive Eliot, not Eliot the shaper of the poem. The speaker is old, dry, philosophic, religious, and most important, a poet. And while the end of his reflections may be predictable in the broadest sense, the manner of their unfolding is not. The emotions which call forth the speaker's reflections are the opposite of certainty. Uncertainty and doubt, along with confusion and regret, lie behind the words of the *Quartets*. If any single characteristic of the speaker's mind can be said to generate and account for his long meditation, it is regret. It is the vague and tantalizing "what might have been" which impels the speaker at the opening of the poem. And at the conclusion of the poem, the speaker's obsession with "what might have been" is joined with the same tormented concern with what was. This concern is described in the words of his dead master as:

> the rending pain of re-enactment
> Of all that you have done, and been; the shame
> Of motives late revealed, and the awareness
> Of things ill done and done to others' harm
> Which once you took for exercise of virtue. (p. 142)[3]

This generative impulse behind the speaker's reflections creates a tone of insistence. What has been, what one did, what one would have done—they cannot all be meaningless. These things cannot all be swept into insignificant oblivion. Yet this solemn desire to find out "what will

[3] All page references following quotations are to T. S. Eliot, *The Complete Poems and Plays*, 1909-1950 (New York, 1962).

suffice" is carried out by a man full of doubt—doubt even about his own work with words. The man's efforts to comprehend the meaning of experience is compared to the poet's effort with language—

> and every attempt
> Is a wholly new start, and a different kind of failure
> Because one has only learnt to get the better of words
> For the thing one no longer has to say. . . .   (p. 128)

The tentativeness and doubt in the *Quartets* begins in the opening lines, and once established does not completely disappear until the end of the poem. The "perhaps," "if," "what might have been," and "to what purpose I do not know" of the opening are reinforced at various times in the poem by the speaker's questions. And self-deprecating assertions such as "that was one way of putting it—not very satisfactory," "twenty years largely wasted," and phrases like "I do not know much about gods," "It seems," and "I sometimes wonder" continue the tone of tentativeness in later sections. This diffidence on the part of the poet has seemed esthetically inconsistent to some readers who have charged Eliot with lapses in his poetic power and with heavy-handed didacticism, or have devised ingenious explanations to account for such a tone. But there is no inherent contradiction in a speaker who is both assertive and diffident. Although the central tenet of the speaker's belief is the incarnation, he is not at all certain just what this belief means. He describes it as "The hint half guessed, the gift half understood" (p. 136). Like Gerontion, he moves through his own memories and history knowing that there are "cunning passages, contrived corridors and issues," and that he can be misled and deceived by vanity and ambition.

The very length of the *Quartets* gives the reflections of the speaker a sense of determined patience; and the wistful, melancholic dwelling on past experiences adds to that sense of resigned persistence a kind of desperation. Eliot makes the reflections of the poem seem experiences of the most serious, of an almost despairing, nature. The description of these experiences further adds a *tristia* because they can neither be fully described nor understood. Like the suffering that led Celia Copplestone to her death:

> . . . such experience can only be hinted at
> In myths and images. To speak about it
> We talk of darkness, labyrinths, Minotaur terrors.   (p. 384)

Each quartet has its own ghostly visitors—the children of the rose garden, the dancing Elyots of "East Coker," the wives and Krishna of "The Dry Salvages," and the dead master of the final quartet. The speaker summons up these specters, much as he recalls the locales around which his thoughts turn, in order to find in them some meaning which he has not been able to grasp. And in this process the reader is held by the speaker almost as tenaciously as the Ancient Mariner holds his wedding guest.

There is an obvious note of a man giving directions: "*There* we have been," "Here is a place of disaffection," "Descend lower," "This is the one way, and the other/Is the same." This quality of pointing, instructing, giving exact directions on how to make a journey, however, is something that progressively involves the reader. By the time the speaker has arrived (with the reader) at his final locale ("Little Gidding"), his earnestness in providing not only directions but a commentary on side effects and mental states reaches its climax. When he is describing the hermitage at "Little Gidding," he combines insistence, tentativeness, doubt, and obsession by repeating six times (with slight change) the single phrase "If you came this way."

This note of obsession in the speaker is common elsewhere in Eliot, and the speaker shares this characteristic with some of the most striking figures in Eliot's later poems and plays. In *The Family Reunion* Eliot uses the phrase the "elected one" to describe Harry—a man suddenly compelled to assume the burden of finding purpose and meaning in life. The speaker of *Ash-Wednesday,* the magus of "Journey of the Magi," Simeon, Celia in *The Cocktail Party,* and most relevant to the *Quartets,* Thomas à Becket, are all elected ones.

Eliot gives no precise explanation of what experiences or attitudes lead such figures to pursue their new way of life. The individual is mysteriously called, and he turns, and thereafter seeks or suffers according to some incomprehensible higher law. As Harry explains—

> my business is not to run away, but to pursue,
> Not to avoid being found, but to seek.
> I would not have chosen this way, had there been any other!
> It is at once the hardest thing, and the only thing possible.
> (p. 208)

Harry is brought to his change of heart by guilt over the death of his wife and by a sense that the world is insane. What this specifically means for the poet of the *Quartets* is uncertain, but the images, conditions and places Harry names as outside the world of insanity are very similar to images, conditions and places that appear in the *Quartets*. Harry's goal is—

> the worship in the desert, the thirst and deprivation,
> A stony sanctuary and a primitive altar,
> The heat of the sun and the icy vigil.   (p. 281)

The character in Eliot that casts most light on the speaker of the *Quartets* is Becket. The fact that "Burnt Norton" began with material left over from *Murder in the Cathedral* suggests the proximity of the two works. The persistence with which the Archbishop contemplates his martyrdom is hardly less intense than the persistence with which the poet contemplates the Logos. What martyrdom means for Becket, purgation and perception mean for the poet. Granted that the Archbishop faced a bloody death and the poet faces impotent old age, that the former ends life with a bang and the latter ends his meditation with a whisper. Nevertheless, what happens in Becket's mind as he contemplates martyrdom bears some analogy to what happens in the poet's mind as he contemplates time, suffering, guilt, and eternity.

Eliot takes care to distinguish between the saint and the ordinary man, and the speaker of the *Quartets* is depicted as an ordinary man:

> But to apprehend
> The point of intersection of the timeless
> With time, is an occupation for the saint—
> No occupation either, but something given
> And taken, in a lifetime's death in love,
> Ardour and selflessness and self-surrender.
> For most of us, there is only the unattended
> Moment, the moment in and out of time.   (p. 136)

The speaker of the *Quartets* is much closer to the chorus than Becket, in some respects. The words Becket addresses to the chorus are, in fact, the words the bird addresses to the speaker at the opening of "Burnt Norton" (p. 118, p. 209).

The speaker, like Becket, knows and believes. But, also like Becket, he must know when to act and when not to act, and he must act for the right motive. To know something does not necessarily assure that one will act rightly. Becket's tempters know more than he does. The Devil can quote scripture, and the First Tempter quotes to the Archbishop almost the exact words the Archbishop used a short time before, addressing the women of the Chorus:

> You know and do not know, what it is to act or suffer
> You know and do not know, what is suffering,
>
> And suffering action. Neither does the actor suffer
> Nor the patient act. Both are fixed
> In an eternal action, an eternal patience
> To which all must consent that it may be willed
> And which all must suffer that they may will it,
> That the pattern may subsist, that the wheel may turn and still
> Be forever still.   (p. 193)

Becket seeks to perfect his will that the Divine pattern may be fulfilled, and is tested, and, paradoxically, helped in this by four tempters. In the *Quartets,* the speaker's effort to understand perfection of will becomes explicit to him as he contemplates four views of time. In some instances the saint and the poet are faced with a parallel dilemma. The first three tempters all want Becket to take a false view of time. The first two want him to relive the past, "For the good times past that are come again/I am your man," says the First Tempter. The second wants him to regain the power of the past by regaining the chancellorship. And the Third Tempter asks him to shape the future according to his own desires by joining with the barons. The speaker in the *Quartets* is similarly faced with the dilemma of how to use time. "What might have been," torments him in "Burnt Norton"; the apparent simplicity and virtue of earlier ages momentarily attracts him in "East Coker." The ceaseless wasting away and death of earth and man appall him in "The Dry Salvages." And even after he has perceived the necessity of detachment in grasping the Divine Logos, he must guard against letting this aloofness become indifference.

Becket is a medieval saint, the speaker of the *Four Quartets* is a 20th century poet, but the saint contemplating martyrdom and the poet's exploring mind both seek right action. The search for right action in Eliot's poetry has been extended from those incapable of action (Prufrock and Gerontion) through the maimed figure of *The Waste Land,* whose final desire is to "at least set my lands in order," to the explicitly religious acceptance of "Because I do not hope to turn." Becket's greatest temptation was the right action for the wrong reason. Thus, something like a whole lifetime of attempted action, of inaction, and of temptation would appear to lie behind the words of the

Quartets. And although Becket's struggle is objectively dramatized with
tempters, there is no less of a struggle represented in the testing of the
speaker's thoughts in the *Quartets* as he works toward his observation
that "the fire and the rose are one."

No small part of the character of the speaker of the *Quartets* is that
of a man wrestling with his own thoughts and emotions like the poet's
"intolerable wrestling with words"—thoughts and emotions which mis-
lead, are vague, slip away, make the speaker feel he knows and does not
know. Although the chief analogy Eliot uses to explain this action is
that of the poet struggling with his material, he had earlier dramatized
comparable mental action by the contest between the conscience of a
man and four tempters.

The speaker has a sense of audience which also may owe something
to *Murder in the Cathedral.* It is, in fact, this sense of audience (or
reader, or auditor) which gives to the speaker's meditations the tone of
public utterance. In the *Quartets,* as in a dramatic monologue, the
reader is crucial to the speaker, but unlike a monologue, there seems to
be no audience inside the poem itself. Nevertheless, the reader is
understood to be extremely close to the speaker—almost as close as
Becket is to his chorus. Whether we are to feel that the poet is
addressing a friend, a fellow religious, or the ideal reader of his poetry—
it makes little difference. All that is necessary is that we see the
closeness between speaker and reader.

Throughout the poem the "you" is assumed to be concerned with
the speaker. The speaker seems to take the rôle of an older guide
conducting a tour of the landscape of the Logos, and much of the
geography he covers is very personal and private. The poet has already
been somewhere, and as he contemplates the place where he has been,
he is involved in a new journey for understanding. And in this he takes
the reader with him:

> I can only say, *there* we have been: but I cannot say where.
> And I cannot say how long, for that is to place it in time.
>
> (p. 119)

At the outset the poet tells his reader that the experience of listening to
these reflections is in itself analogous to the experience which lies
behind the reflections. As the poet ponders "what might have been,"
for example, he breaks off his thought to address the reader:

> Footfalls echo in the memory
> Down the passage we did not take

> Towards the door we never opened
> Into the rose-garden. My words echo
> Thus, in your mind.
>   But to what purpose
> Disturbing the dust on a bowl of rose-leaves
> I do not know.   (p. 117)

The speaker breaks the progress of his thought to tell the reader that listening is comparable to attempting to grasp the meaning of "what might have been." Just as the uncertainty of "But to what purpose ... I do not know" helps to define the speaker's personality, so his attention to the reader helps establish the dramatic insistence of his thoughts.

The poet's attention to his reader alters slightly from *Quartet* to *Quartet,* and we will treat these changes shortly, but first we must try to answer the second, and more difficult, of our two questions: How is the thought of the speaker appropriate to his character? Or, to put it another way, how are the speaker's tentativeness, his doubt, his obsessions—with his material and with his reader—reflected in his thought? Or, to put it most simply: What characterizes the thought of the *Quartets*?

One of the first things that strike the reader about the ordering of the speaker's thought is its similarities with the ordering of action in *The Waste Land*. Both poems begin with an experience of ecstasy—or near ecstasy; the one in the hyacinth garden, the other with the rose garden. And both end in the vicinity of places of prayer—chapel perilous and "Little Gidding." There are also the similarities in the five-fold structure of both poems—with parts three, four and five in both poems apparently serving comparable functions. Finally, there is in both poems a clear sense of moving toward a goal, a sense of spiritual quest. Both are mental journeys—the one rendered more in cultural, literary, mythic terms; the other, almost entirely in religious terms.

Trying to describe the thought of the *Quartets* poses two separate problems. One is: why *four* poems? The other is the ordering of thought in each separate *Quartet*. Naturally the two questions become joined at a number of points, but we can at least begin to answer them separately.

We have already speculated that the four views of time represented by the four *Quartets* are confronted by the speaker so that he may know how to act. It is only the fourth view that enables him to understand how he should regard the dilemma of time and eternity. The speaker finds that he cannot rest in the first three views—nor even in the fourth; but with the view of "Little Gidding" attained, the speaker can perceive something new in his point of departure, and he is at least enabled to complete a cycle by going back to where he started. He has attained the knowledge which makes right action possible:

> And the end of all our exploring
> Will be to arrive where we started
> And know the place for the first time.   (p. 145)

Individually the four poems represent four basic perceptions of time. Although the poet's time sense in "Burnt Norton" is the least definite of the four—he sees the manor house as a vague symbol of time's passage—the time at the opening seems related first to the old house and garden and then to memories of youthful joy. (And there is here even the distant hope that he might somehow recapture this joy connected with children.) Certainly, "Burnt Norton" is dominated by private memories of what happened, what did not, and what might have happened, whereas in "East Coker" there is more concern with family and racial origins—not with an individual's memory but with familial beginnings. If the family garden typifies "Burnt Norton," the village green, a communal civilization, marks the locale of "East Coker." "Burnt Norton" makes the poet think of the philosophical and theological dilemmas resulting from God's omnipotence and man's limitation, from the relationship between the eternal *nunc* of God and man's past-present-future view of time. "East Coker" calls the poet's attention to man's time, to the time of *generation,* to the appropriate time, the right time in which the right action is carried out. This movement, from concerns most immediately related to the speaker—questions of what did affect and what might have affected his life—to temporal rhythms more distant although strongly present in his own life, continues in successive *Quartets.* The poet seems to view each locale as approaching closer to antiquity—even to eternity. In "East Coker" we are in the presence of generations—country time, ancestral time, a time of seasons, milking, coupling. In "The Dry Salvages" we are made aware of the presence of gods always felt within us: "a time/Older than that of chronometers, older/Than time counted by anxious worried women." And, strangely, this *Quartet* which begins with the oldest known time is dominated by a sense of futurity. The senses of past and future are joined—the future is "a faded rose." And in "Little Gidding" we are beyond even the sea's time or the time of gods, we are in God's time, everything is now, a moment, present: "suspended in time between pole and tropic,"

> There is no earth smell
> Or smell of living thing. This is the spring time
> But not in time's covenant.   (p. 138)

The season of "Little Gidding" is not in itself old, but the speaker perceives its eternity. This capability allows the poet to see past, present and future as interrelated parts of a tapestry upon which the viewer moves. The speaker moves through psychological, historical and mythical perspectives to a mystical awareness of the timelessness of time. But this simplicity is deceptive. Although each starting point is characterized by a clear enough perspective, within each *Quartet* all four perspectives are touched on and the religious point of view is a constant. But the religious view which is only briefly stressed in "Burnt Norton" becomes more important in successive *Quartets*.

The movement of thought within each *Quartet* is fairly uniform. In each first movement the speaker deals with the conception of time which he cannot fully keep or finally understand. The second movements recount a search for a new understanding apparently required because of the speaker's inability to retain or hold the original conception. By the end of this movement the poet reaches new insights—insights which he pursues in Part III. The third movements describe this exploration in a combination of journey metaphors and reflections on spiritual states of purgation and selflessness. In the fourth section, the speaker ponders and prays—each fourth movement seems to be a religious formulation in light of death. The final sections are all codas—usually returning to the opening conception—the fourth, "Little Gidding," returning in imagery to "Burnt Norton."

In sum: each *Quartet* presents the speaker following an almost ritualistic sequence of insight, loss, searching, praying, and an ending in climactic perception. This movement in each *Quartet*—even so vaguely outlined—suggests the kind of psychological stages ordinarily associated with mystical experience. It is curious that Evelyn Underhill, trying to draw a "composite portrait" of the development of mystical awareness, decided that such experiences might best be divided into five stages, curious because the five stages bear some similarities to the five parts of each *Quartet*. Underhill's phases occur in "the movement of consciousness from lower to higher levels of reality." Very briefly the five passages are: 1) an awakening to Divine reality marked by "joy and exaltation," 2) the realization of imperfection and an attempt to eliminate by discipline and mortification all that stands in the way of progress towards God, 3) purgation bringing illumination, 4) the purification of self—mystic pain or mystic death. The self becomes "utterly passive," 5) union—"The establishment of life upon transcendent levels of reality...."[4]

Eliot in his Preface to St.-John Perse's *Anabase* said: "There is a logic of the imagination as well as a logic of concepts."[5] The imaginative logic of the *Quartets* is based on a movement—which becomes by its fourth repetition almost a ritual drama of stages, observations, and perceptions analogous to the phases mystics pass through on their way to enlightenment.

The speaker's search for love traces a course "As in the figure of the ten stairs" (p. 122). The mysticism of the *Quartets* is not like that of John of the Cross or the Buddha—but it draws on them and others, and adds some distinct Eliotic touches. Its illuminations seem more poetic than religious, its way is more programmatic ("prayer, observance, discipline, thought and action") than ecstatic, but its stages are fairly clear—its goal just as certain as that of John of the Cross. The *Quartets* has none of the passionate excesses of *The Ascent to Mount Carmel,* but its English reserve and rationality might make it appropriate to have sub-titled it: "The Ascent to Little Gidding."

Now to look more closely at the movement of thought in each *Quartet.*

"Burnt Norton" opens with the speaker contemplating time as past-present-future for man, but as an eternal now for God. If time is an eternal *nunc,* then it would seem everything is determined, even predetermined, and speculation about "what might have been" pointless. The Christian answer to this dilemma is given by both Becket and his tempter in lines we have already quoted from *Murder in the Cathedral.* In that play Eliot explained that all are "fixed/In an eternal action . . . / To which all must consent that it may be willed,/And which all must suffer that they may will it." But the poet of the *Quartets* cannot yet will his predetermined part in the fixed timelessness of God. What kinds of things the speaker thinks and what he feels as he seeks to consent, seeks to will his part in the eternal action, are the matter of the *Quartets.* At the outset the speaker cannot even concentrate on the flat, abstract Boethian view of time. His emotional state (perhaps regret) will not permit that. He has his memories ("Footfalls echo in the memory") and they overtake and overwhelm him. Conveniently, too, because his enticement into his formative memories and world of persistent desires neatly dramatizes how the past (memories) controls future (desires) and perpetually exists in the present—almost whether we would invoke

---

[4] Evelyn Underhill, *Mysticism* (New York, 1955), pp. 168-70.
[5] *Collected Poems* (Princeton, 1971), p. 676.

these memories or not. They are there and they shape our lives. And, furthermore, the memory sequence illustrates how the richest sense of reality is achieved by losing all sense of time, by returning to "our first garden." But by the end of the first movement the poet comes to the anguished awareness that he cannot find a method of holding past and future together by plunging into the recesses of his own past. "Go, go, go, said the bird: Human kind cannot bear very much reality." One must find other means for holding memory and desire in balance. Even the abstract formulation is better because less deeply felt:

> Time past and time future
> What might have been and what has been
> Point to one end, which is always present.   (p. 118)

Deprived of the consolation of personal memory, the poet turns outward toward nature. In trying to reconcile God's timelessness and man's past-present-future, he observes some patterns of reconciliation offered by nature. One pattern is physical juxtaposition—like garlic next to sapphires—another is the healed wound, another is perception of analogies between man and nature, still another is the perception of connection among such diverse things as boarhound, boars and stars. The progression of thought couched in the intricate auditory pattern and tetrameter lines of the opening of the second movement is abruptly shifted by the free verse phrases—"At the still point of the turning world." But the phrase seems to be a perception that springs out of the preceding reconciliations, balances, or patterns just formulated. It seems fairly clear that the speaker is describing a perception which climaxes the chain of patterns, the ordering of all contraries—namely, the perception of time still and still moving "Where past and future are gathered." The poet bluntly says he has had this perception, and has experienced the fullest sense of harmony and reconciliation. He has had experiences of the timeless in time, and the essence of those experiences is the momentary reconciliation of all contraries. In a further explanation of this state he describes in detail the feelings that accompany such an enlightenment: freedom, release, a sense of grace, a completion of ecstasy, a resolution of horror.

The conclusion of this moment of incomparable enlightenment is, however, strangely similar to the conclusion of the imaginative leap into memory. Once again the meditation ends with the awareness that human kind cannot bear the full realization of most intense awareness, we cannot comprehend timelessness:

> the enchainment of past and future
> Woven in the weakness of the changing body,
> Protects mankind from heaven and damnation
> Which flesh cannot endure.   (p. 119)

The summary of the second movement redefines consciousness
much as the end of the first movement redefined reality. Consciousness
becomes the perception of the still point. Looking back to the beginning it is memory, "the moment in the rose garden," looking forward
to "Little Gidding," "The moment in the draughty church at smokefall." The right use of memory is as a storehouse of such personal and
historical moments, and such moments, the poet tentatively concludes,
can only be gained by an absorption in time: "Only through time time
is conquered."

The third movement dramatizes this immersion in time by describing the descent in terms of a tube journey and then didactically
pointing out how this journey must be one of complete purgation, and
"not in movement/But abstention from movement" (p. 121).

The poet muses in the fourth part on the possible endings of
life—his and the reader's—after "our day" is ended. A strong sensation
conveyed by the puzzling lines is that of enclosure in the grave, but the
enclosure (of tendril and spray, and the chilled fingers of yew) is
softened by the question format. Eliot's theology in the last lines turns
on a pun, a pun he will use again. He says that after men die, the light
of beauty and awareness is—"*still*/At the still point." Without movement? Or, continuing? Apparently both. A rich but light assertion of
belief:

> After the kingfisher's wing
> Has answered light to light, and is silent, the light is still
> At the still point of the turning world.   (p. 121)

The fifth movement begins by treating the doubt hovering around
still. One still point does not a reconciliation make. There has to be a
design, a total plan of which the still point is a part. The poet amplifies
this belief with several images drawn from literature and music, art
(Chinese jar) and dance. The initial formulation is clearest:

> Words, after speech, reach
> Into the silence. Only by the form, the pattern,
> Can words or music reach
> That stillness, as a Chinese jar still
> Moves perpetually in its stillness.   (p. 121)

It is only in the form of art that words, or perceptions, assume the stillness and movement of immortal voice—or movement. This is the first of many analogies the searching mind of the poet will fashion in order to convey a living, moving, growing understanding of the "still point" perception.

All the previous attempts at grasping relations between past and future, memory and desire, individual insight and the universal pattern are summed up in the concluding part of the fifth movement. No totally new ideas are explored but some things earlier touched on are developed. At the outset, for example, present, past, future were seen in terms of speech: "My words echo/Thus, in your mind" (p. 117). Among the several imagistic analogies helping us apprehend the idea of time as the eternal *nunc*, the analogies with speech, literature and poetry are most fully developed. These figures develop the earlier "still point of the turning world" model, providing metaphoric equivalents in such things as the spoken word eternally held in form (literature) and visual movement caught in spatial form (the Chinese jar). The enigmatic fourth movement—the premonition of death—is somewhat clarified by the plight of the living *logos*, the human embodiment of "the still point of the turning world":

> The Word in the desert
> Is most attacked by voices of temptation,
> The crying shadow in the funeral dance,
> The loud lament of the disconsolate chimera.   (p. 122)

The Word in the desert is like the poet in the process of meditation (and like Becket facing his martyrdom). Thus the doubt and questioning expressed in Part Four is analogous to the temptation the Word undergoes at "the funeral dance."

The final contemplation of time, movement, pattern in the last 17 lines seems to place the abstractions love and desire into the visual, still point pattern of reconciled time. Desire is the turning world; love is at its unmoving center:

> Desire itself is movement
> Not in itself desirable;
> Love is itself unmoving,
> Only the cause and end of movement.   (p. 122)

There is now expressed the awareness of how the imaginative plunge into the rose garden—which the speaker earlier found unendurable—

must not only be endured but must be seized as the center around which his life turns. Love ("Timeless, and undesiring/Except in the aspect of time") and desire, the impulse toward futurity ("movement/ Not in itself desirable"), must constantly be joined in the now. The poet does not know in the first movement what will come of his meditation—"But to what purpose/Disturbing the dust on a bowl of rose leaves? I do not know." At the conclusion of his meditation he is ready to perceive love in time. He does not ponder the meaning of the disturbed dust; he apprehends while the dust moves. Memory and desire are reconciled in the *Now*:

> Sudden in a shaft of sunlight
> Even while the dust moves
> There rises the hidden laughter.   (p. 122)

He has, in the course of meditating on relationships and accepting the present, been able to perceive like a child—timelessly:

> Quick now, here, now, always—
> Ridiculous the waste sad time
> Stretching before and after.   (p. 122)

The abstract formulations of past, present and future are likewise found ridiculous. Time is redeemed (psychologically at least) by accepting memory (past) while one moves toward desire (future) controlled by love (the constant now of the present). This perception will not be substantially altered in successive quartets. It will be tested, weighed, and enriched, however, in prolonged meditation.

The poet is apparently in or near the village of his ancestors, "East Coker," when he speaks the opening words of the second *Quartet*: "In my beginning is my end." The movement of this *Quartet*, like "Burnt Norton," turns on a full understanding of this opening phrase. Among the implications of the opening word is the truism that our ancestors have determined our fate. The final words of the poem are the motto of Mary Queen of Scots. "In my end is my beginning"—with its religious implications of life beginning at death.

The speaker's attitude toward his reader, or auditor, is not as intimate here as in "Burnt Norton." There is less a tone of "shall we follow," more a tone of an experienced traveler informing the inexperienced, the father speaking to the son, teacher to pupil. But the invitation the poet gives is gentle, subtle. After he has established the rhythm of generations rising and falling, the rhythm of man's struggles and failures, he carefully describes the exact route and the exact features of the approach to the village. There is almost a tone of warning and a feeling of irresistible attraction. You must be careful, "You lean against a bank while a van passes," and you cannot turn back:

> the deep lane insists on the direction
> Into the village, in the electric heat
> Hypnotised.   (p. 123)

And viewers must keep things in a certain perspective; we must keep a distance:

> In that open field
> If you do not come too close, if you do not come too close,
> On a summer midnight you can hear the music
> Of the weak pipe and little drum . . .   (pp. 123-124)

What we see and hear and are told about is the time of ancestors, the rhythm of an older and more ordered society, the rituals of a rustic and agricultural world. But, as in the imaginative flight of "Burnt Norton," the speaker cannot possess this experience. "Dawn points," "The dawn wind/Wrinkles," He is "here/Or there, or elsewhere." He is "In my beginning." As we learn from the next movement, the past cannot be held as an unchanging guide. Here, however, his retreat into the past is not accompanied by any clear assertion that he finds unbearable the imagined rustic order. He recognizes the integrity of its rhythms, but the meaning of that time simply escapes him. Wisdom fades and disappears no matter how vividly it has been felt. At the end of the first movement the speaker is still beginning—the world which has passed, the world of the past, has no immediate value to him:

> I am here
> Or there, or elsewhere. In my beginning.   (p. 124)

The familial rhythms and rituals, "The rhythm in their dancing/Or in their living in the living season," have not been transmitted.

The second movement opens with 17 lines of strangely archaic tetrameter (which Eliot calls "a worn out poetical fashion"). The rustic rhythms of the first movements here give way to nature's rhythms that have not observed their expected order. To grasp the meaning of rhythms and rituals observed by previous generations and now lost, the poet contemplates, as it were, the broken and inevitable breaking of the great rhythms of seasons and cosmic cycles:

> The disturbance of the spring
> And creatures of the summer heat,
> And snowdrops writhing under feet.   (p. 124)

The course of other unobserved rhythms is traced to the ultimate disturbance:

> That shall bring
> The world to that destructive fire
> Which burns before the ice-cap reigns.   (p. 125)

In the second part of the second movement the poet calls attention to the style of his preceding lines and makes his point clearly and simply: "It was not (to start again) what one had expected." The most moving insight into the past does not have the expected effect; the inevitable end one postulates for the world is not "what one might have expected." This section then goes on more concretely to describe how age is not what is expected, how experience does not help, and how there is no "end" in the spirit's journey to understanding. Rather the whole journey is

> in a dark wood, in a bramble,
> On the edge of a grimpen, where is no secure foothold,
> And menaced by monsters, fancy lights,
> Risking enchantment.   (p. 125)

Again, it is at the conclusion of the second movement that the poet grasps what is necessary when history, experience, and life slip away from us:

> The only wisdom we can hope to acquire
> Is the wisdom of humility: humility is endless.
>
> The houses are all gone under the sea.
>
> The dancers are all gone under the hill.   (p. 126)

Humility (like love earlier) is a virtue prerequisite to perception of the still point. It negates the disappearance of the Elyot family and even the worse disorders of nature. It is part of the center holding the wheel of past and future in harmony; it puts the mind in tune with eternity; it "is endless."

The third movement is devoted to the attainment of humility (as in "Burnt Norton," the third movement describes the pursuit of the here and now). Eliot begins by giving us the sense of all men passing into death and then, by his prayer—"I said to my soul, be still, and let the dark come upon you/Which shall be the darkness of God," we see that the first thing necessary is the full acceptance of death. This acceptance is revealed in the *waiting*. When one thus waits, the great transmutation occurs: "So the darkness shall be the light, and the stillness the dancing." The insight of "Burnt Norton" is thus equated with the virtues of "East Coker." Eliot concludes the third movement, after giving some images of this ecstatic transformation and repeating the necessity for waiting in humility, with a series of exhortations that might have come from *The Ascent of Mount Carmel*:

> In order to arrive at what you do not know
>   You must go by a way which is the way of ignorance.
> In order to possess what you do not possess
>   You must go by way of dispossession.

The fourth movement returns to a "periphrastic . . . worn-out poetic fashion" comparable to the beginning of the second movement. And in a sense the reader who can say the prayer couched in the allegorical didacticism and the derivative metaphysical manner of these stanzas has already demonstrated humility, his ability to take the negative way. The lesson of the fourth movement is clear: we must accept suffering and we must accept the spiritual authority of traditional religion:

> Wherein, if we do well, we shall
> Die of the absolute paternal care
> That will not leave us, but prevents us everywhere.

The summary, the fifth movement, once again pulls together the reflections, insights and conclusions of the previous movements. Art and poetry provide the key metaphors. The poet tells us he is in "the middle way," neither beginning nor ending. And although he is always beginning, the knowledge and beliefs he now holds make him *feel* as though he were in "the middle way." For he is ever the writer who learns to use language only when he is no longer disposed to say it in the manner he has so painfully learned. At the outset the rhythms of the past escaped us; at the conclusion all of our struggling reveals that there is only the fight to recover what has been lost. And found and lost again and again . . .

> And what there is to conquer
> By strength and submission, has already been discovered
> Once or twice, or several times, by men whom one cannot hope
> To emulate—but there is no competition—
> For us, there is only the trying.
> The rest is not our business.   (p. 128)

In this view of life as a continual series of beginnings, home is not the place of our ancestors—it is "where one starts from" and what one starts with. The whole baggage of inheritance is summed up in what we are at each beginning, nothing more. In this process, age and the memory of the dead make beginnings more complicated, more difficult. Not even the consolations of "Burnt Norton," the spots of time, the still point, not even having grasped the *here* and *now* ("Quick now, here, now, always—") suffices to keep one beginning. It is humility supported by conviction (gained by reflecting on those who have lived before us) that teaches:

> We must be still and still moving
> Into another intensity
> For further union, a deeper communion
> Through the dark cold and empty desolation,
> The wave cry, the wind cry, the vast waters
> Of the petrel and the porpoise.

There is no ending. The informed life is continually beginning: "In my end is my beginning." The greatest beginning is death.

True to the wisdom of "East Coker" that calls for another intensity and ends with "The wave cry, the wind cry," the beginning of "The Dry Salvages" takes up such a new intensity. In one way "The Dry Salvages" is itself a terminus for meditations on time. For the river and the sea represent what "is and was from the beginning." In terms of human life there is nothing older. After "The Dry Salvages" the penetration into time stops; the reader must move out of time.

The poet, in the first movement of "The Dry Salvages," does not, as he has done previously, ask us to follow him into a garden, or station us somewhere and tell us to listen and watch. He assumes that his descriptions of river and sea will result in his reader's recognizing these forces within himself. He is not talking about formative memories, or family and racial beginnings (although both are included in this section); he is rather reminding us that "The river is within us, the sea is all about us." His object, through his images and rhythms, is to make the reader feel this, and then to tell him what this antiquity means for man.

The humility and faith of "East Coker" have brought the poet to seek "another intensity," but as in the previous *Quartets,* the new perception is overwhelming. He is plunged and plunges us into the rhythms and pulses of water. The only measurer of this time is the bell—constantly beginning and ending:

> The tolling bell
> Measures time not our time, rung by the unhurried
> Ground swell. . . .   (p. 131)

Here one is inundated with the sense of perpetual movement, destruction, addition, age, meaningless inhuman (unredeemable) time. It can only lead the poet (and implicitly the reader with him) to be wearied, almost appalled at the ageless repetition and sequences. Thus in the modified sestina of the second movement the poet plaintively asks: "Where is there an end of it?" Eventually, there is something absurd about a philosophy of eternal beginnings. One cannot go on forever. "There is no end, but addition," hopelessly says the poet in the second stanza, only "Years of living among the breakage." The final addition of age is the most hopeless change, for the rhythm of the bell goes on endlessly:

> We cannot think of a time that is oceanless
> Or of an ocean not littered with wastage
> Or of a future that is not liable
> Like the past, to have no destination.   (p. 132)

There is no end, the poet concludes, except "Only the hardly, barely prayable/Prayer of the one Annunciation." The only escape is the miracle of the Incarnation. Humility has led to faith. No philosophy of time can satisfy the speaker, only a faith that the Eternal has somehow taken on flesh.

In the second movement he now turns to reconsider a way of perceiving the "sudden illumination." The poet had explored these moments earlier in a similar prosaic section in the second movement of "Burnt Norton." Now he recalls this: "I have said before/That the past experience of one life only but of many generations—. . . ."

He had not said it in that way. It was not so obvious, at least, that he conceived of the "still point" as the meaning of experience. Nor had he at that time been so clear that the still point gathered the experience of many rather than that of one. He further develops his thinking by adding that these moments of illumination are as much involved with agony as with the ecstasy that he had previously emphasized. At the end of the second movement he provides another analogous image for the "still point at the turning world." Here the image of the meaning gathered from the agonizing experiences is that of "the ragged rock in the restless water." "The Dry Salvages" themselves become a symbol of permanence in change of that which is "still and still moving":

> On a halcyon day it is merely a monument,
> In navigable weather it is always a seamark
> To lay a course by: but in the sombre season
> Or the sudden fury, is what it always was.   (p. 133)

What the rock always was, was a ragged rock. This memory of a constant object assuming many aspects and functions lingers on in the mind of the speaker as he opens the third movement. Time like the rock remains constant and manifests pastness and futurity according to the circumstances of those beholding it.

In both of the previous *Quartets* the third movement pursued further the ideas that had been arrived at by the end of the second movement. In both instances the exploration was expressed in metaphors of a journey. "Burnt Norton" had the tube descent; in "East Coker" the eminent and the petty passed before the eyes of the poet into the word of death. In "The Dry Salvages" the poet describes the experience of others who journey. But they who leave are not they who arrive. There is no past behind them or future before them—unlike "The Dry Salvages," where the past and future around the self are analogous to sea rocks with the oceans all about them. The rocks, like the self, have a different appearance for each day. They change with the changing sea. The appearance of the rocks is determined by the mood of the waters, and in certain seasons they are always the same: "The way up is the way down; the way forward is the way back." The still point of this turning world, the pile of rocks, is still and still moving.

But the main reflection of this view of time in the third movement

comes in Krishna's words to Arjuna urging him to act disinterestedly
without regard to past or future. What "disinterestedly" means finally
must wait for the third movement of "Little Gidding." For Krishna
"the illusion of going forward is all that we have in this incomprehensible life. But it is a necessary illusion. The Buddha has said that the
true man is the one who is willing to remain suspended between the
unknown shore that he started from and the unknowable shore he is
moving toward. . . . This is also the Hindu doctrine of *Karma*."[6] And it
is also a quality of that right action which the speaker seeks.

In a sense the third movement is an ingenious collation of parallel
religious sentiments from Buddhism and Hinduism, sentiments which
are indistinguishable from the views of Christian mystics. These religious views anticipate the fourth movement in particular as well as the
view of the entire fourth *Quartet*. It is as though Eliot were saying in
"The Dry Salvages" that the unutterable antiquity of the sea calls forth,
in an annunciation, the prayer of the fourth movement, and the
extended prayer of "Little Gidding."

The speaker addresses someone at the end of the third movement
(evidently the reader):

> O voyagers, O seamen,
> . . . .
> Not fare well,
> But fare forward, voyagers.   (p. 135)

The real destination is the moment, the present, the act of voyaging—
not any particular land or port.

To guide this voyage the poet invokes the patroness of sailors, the
woman of "the one Annunciation," the medium by which the Incarnation was effected. And in his invocation, comprising the fourth movement, he asks Mary's intercession for the voyagers of Part I, for the sons
of those "anxious waiting women," and for the dead—those beyond
"the sound of the sea bell's/Perpetual angelus" (p. 135).

The poet begins the fifth movement by asserting that the desire to
know the future is common, to be expected, but is usually involved
with cheap sensationalism:

> To explore the womb, or tomb, or dreams; all these are usual
> Pastimes and drugs, and features of the press. . . .   (p. 136)

[6] K. N. Kutty, "The Place of 'The Dry Salvages' in Eliot's *The Four Quartets*."
(An unpublished paper.)

Such searching is idle curiosity—curiosity is, we are told, a crucial part of the view that sees time as past, present and future. A more worthy object of our desire to know would be to learn how to observe time differently:

>   to apprehend
> The point of intersection of the timeless
> With time, is an occupation for the saint. . . .   (p. 136)

Becoming more confident, and insistent to the point of didacticism, the poet resorts to pure statement to explain that for most this apprehension is limited to a brief moment of illumination. Yet these "are only hints and guesses" and the rest is the flat, ordinary "prayer, observance, discipline, thought and action." And of all the hints the Incarnation is the one gift by which we can achieve the reconciliation sought since the opening of "Burnt Norton":

> Here the impossible union
> Of spheres of existence is actual,
> Here the past and future
> Are conquered, and reconciled. . . .   (p. 136)

In the course of exalting the perception of Incarnation, the speaker downgrades the means which he has found (and which most find) necessary for spiritual insight. He describes these means as: "The moment in and out of time,/The distraction fit, lost in a shaft of sunlight. . . ." Such moments, earlier described ecstatically in "Burnt Norton," are now, however, only "hints and guesses" and must be followed by "prayer, observance, discipline, thought and action." Thus might man be truly freed from past and future. But for most "right action" is neither realized nor understood:

>   there is the aim
> Never here to be realised;
> Who are only undefeated
> Because we have gone on trying . . .   (p. 136)

Most are content if their lives (and deaths) have nourished "the life of significant soil."

All the major themes of the *Quartets* have been presented before "Little Gidding." The purpose of this *Quartet* is to further develop some implications of the earlier *Quartets*: "The moment in the draughty church at smokefall" ("Burnt Norton"), the "As we grow older/The world becomes stranger, the pattern more complicated/Of dead and living" ("East Coker"), and the "prayer, observance, discipline, thought and action" which leads to the apprehension of "The point of intersection of the timeless/With time [which] is an occupation for the saint" ("Dry Salvages"). It is this latter theme which best explains the time consciousness with which the fourth *Quartet* opens.

"Little Gidding"'s season of midwinter spring occurs in a particular now, or present, of the ordinary past-present-future world. We are not asked to enter imaginatively into a "first world," nor is there any "earth smell," "dung and death" of ancestral life, nor do we perceive the rhythm of timeless waters within us—we are expected to follow the poet on pilgrimage:

> more intense than the blaze of branch or brazier,
> Stirs the dumb spirit: No wind but pentecostal fire
> In the dark time of the year. Between melting and freezing
> The soul's sap quivers. There is no earth smell
> Or smell of living thing.   (p. 138)

We are told that the spirit stirs, the "soul's sap quivers," and that we are at a world's *end*. Our presence is no longer simply assumed; there is an intensification of master and novice. We are being instructed or initiated, being introduced to holy ground, to a point in time when eternity made its presence felt—to a place (and there are many such places) where past, present and future may be ingathered. Eliot was much more explicit about such places in *Murder in the Cathedral*:

> For the blood of thy martyrs and saints
> Shall enrich the earth, shall create the holy places.
> For wherever a saint has dwelt, wherever a martyr has given
>   his blood . . .
> There is holy ground, and the sanctity shall not depart from it
> Though armies trample over it; though sightseers come
>   with guide-books. . . .   (p. 221)

Like an incantation the poet repeats, "if you came." We are given exact and precise details of how to manage the journey, what to expect, what we must do. And finally, the poet says, "you are here." We must not be there as sightseers, not as members of any army, not

                    to verify
            Instruct yourself, or inform curiosity
            Or carry report. You are here to kneel
            Where prayer has been valid.   (p. 139)

Thus in the first movement we find what we have been led to expect—a
place, a here, now, where time can be seen and experienced under the
eye of eternity. Both the still point found through the meaning of the
agony of others and the dead generations whose rhythms have disap-
peared (of "East Coker") find a voice in this place. The past assumes
meaning and lives, for here "what the dead had no speech for, when
living,/They can tell you, being dead."

We have here not only another analogue for the still point, but the
perception of the saint's view of time which we shall hear "in the
communication/Of the dead . . . tongued with fire beyond the language
of the living." In the apprehension of the meaning of this holy ground
we arrive at the full awareness of time:

            Here, the intersection of the timeless moment
            Is England and nowhere. Never and always.   (p. 139)

The speaker no more than says, "I have brought you to the holy
place, to the living waters, drink and be reborn," and the movement
ends. We are plunged quickly into the "death of hope and despair."
Thus the pattern of the previous *Quartets* continues—the perception of
the first movement is momentary, then disappears. It must be regained
in the second, and when it is regained it is something different which in
turn reveals the need for further effort. The first part of the second
movement is a lyric expressing total destruction, conveying despon-
dency, hopelessness. Earth, air, fire, water become executioners. None
of the incantation and rituals by which the occultists (up to Yeats
himself) sought to restore the soul of the rose from its ashes (what Eliot
calls summoning "the spectre of the rose") are of any use. Death is
death and magic cannot restore an old man:

            Ash on the old man's sleeve
            Is all the ash the burnt roses leave.

The inevitable passing of the material universe mocks our refusal to
recognize the spiritual. His prayer at "Little Gidding" and Yeats' occult
incantations are comparable acts, but neither produces miracles.

In a dramatic shift of style, Eliot, imitating Dante, recounts an hallucinatory moment. Ordinarily we would expect a prosaic analysis following the lyric of the second movement. But we have instead a narrative-dramatic account of the apparition of some dead poet (brown-baked like Dante's purgatorial souls). The promised "communication/ Of the dead" is hardly what one would have imagined. The former master (every master and no specific master) discloses "the gifts reserved for age": "Expiring sense/Without enchantment," "The conscious impotence of rage/At human folly," and "The rending pain of reenactment/Of all you have done, and been" (p. 142). The final message of the spirit ("what the dead had no speech for/When living") is acceptance. And acceptance means purgation: "that refining fire/ Where you must move in measure like a dancer." (Another analogy for the still point of I, ii.) Or, as the poet puts it in "East Coker," this acceptance is to "quake in frigid purgatorial fires/Of which the flame is roses, and the smoke is briars" (p. 128).

The third movement explores the perception that one must live in purgative fires by describing the attitude of mind necessary to this purgation. One must fare forward, but he cannot fare forward with indifference. He must hold a balance between attachment and detachment. If, as we were told, love exists between memory and desire like the still moment of now between past and future, we are also told that that figure may be imperfect if it "imposes a pattern, and falsifies" (p. 125). For the past must provide us with the experiences which will nourish love so that love may become

> unmoving
> Only the cause and end of movement,
> Timeless, and undesiring
> Except in the aspect of time
> Caught in the form of limitation
> Between being and unbeing.   (p. 122)

This is very clear in the third movement of "Little Gidding" where the poet says:

> This is the use of memory:
> For liberation—not less of love but expanding
> Of love beyond desire, and so the liberation
> From the future as well as the past.   (p. 142)

The use of memory has been the motivating force of the reflections in these poems ever since the echoes called the poet back to his first world. Here, after following and exploring its use in numerous ways, he states memory's use—liberation. He further explains this statement with an example seemingly drawn from personal life, and then expands on it by alluding to history—the time and circumstances which produced the ruined hermitage of "Little Gidding." He says a man's interests (literature?) may be the source of a man's love of a country (England?) but that interest comes to be of little importance in his love ("Though never indifferent") as time passes. That with which a love begins goes on to new and different loves, but through memory the original love always remains part of the process and the total memory of that process suggests that the future too may fit into a pattern of love:

> See, now they vanish,
> The faces and places, with the self which, as it could, loved them,
> To become renewed, transfigured, in another pattern.   (p. 142)

Can it be so with history? The mystics would hold it can. Thus the speaker's appropriation of Dame Julian's words which would put even fratricidal wars that destroyed tradition and belief into a divine pattern of love:

> Sin is Behovely, but
> All shall be well, and
> All manner of things shall be well   (pp. 142-143)

Although the speaker was tempted to reject the "wisdom of the old" in "East Coker," he has not repudiated the past entirely. He does, however, question why we should revere the past, or honor one period or age more than another. Why should we think of or celebrate the men of the English civil war? Because they have left us a symbol of attachment (Milton, Charles I) and detachment (Ferrar) which are forms of love—not indifference, "Tumid apathy." History can purify, leaving only the motive, and by that purification the enemies "are folded into a single party" of men who acted out of belief. By this view of history, Eliot thus seeks to reconcile on a social scale what he had reconciled in "Burnt Norton" on an individual level when he saw that "The trilling wire in the blood/Sings below inveterate scars/And reconciles forgotten wars" (p. 118).

The fourth movement is both an interlude and a climax. A climax, because it makes the ultimate theological statement. Each fourth movement is concerned with death, and each is particularly appropriate to the conception of place and time given at the outset of its respective *Quartet*. The fourth movement in "Burnt Norton" is more personal, more concerned with individual doubts; that in "East Coker" is expressed in a theology and allegory appropriate to an agricultural village of the 16th century; the prayer to the Virgin in "The Dry Salvages" is in accord with the traditions of seafaring people who prayed to the Virgin and carved masthead figures of females. Here, once again, a fourth movement is concerned with the timeless moment, the moment of intersection, the moment of release. It announces plainly and clearly that the moment of death will be a release from "sin and error." And in such a belief, the Holy Spirit descending like an enemy plane ("The dove descending breaks the air/With flames of incandescent terror") becomes the spirit of release. The tortuous route from the deterministic expression of past, present and future at the opening of "Burnt Norton" is here completed. If time cannot be redeemed, man can be redeemed. His action is to choose the right action by submission (purgation, humility, detachment, the right use of memory):

> The only hope, or else despair
> Lies in the choice of pyre or pyre—
> To be redeemed from fire to fire.   (p. 144)

The agent of this redemption is Love—even if it be love like Hercules' bride Deianeria who, though misled, gave Hercules the shirt of flame which was supposed to win his unending devotion. Hercules escaped the shirt of flame only by killing himself on a pyre:

> Who then devised the torment? Love,
> Love is the unfamiliar name
> Behind the hands that wove
> The intolerable shirt of flame
> Which human power cannot remove.
> We only live, only suspire
> Consumed by either fire or fire.

The fifth movement is a recapitulation of "Little Gidding" and the whole poem. Here are those elements from the previous *Quartets* most worthy of the emphatic position at the close of a long and involved work. Everything that is in this part of the poem has appeared elsewhere. One of the main problems of understanding this section is to determine the rationale for the speaker's choice.

The poet has shifted his attitude toward his reader in the course of the *Quartets* and although these shifts are most immediately noticeable at the outset of each *Quartet*, the change in attitude is especially noticeable in this final section. In the conclusion of "Burnt Norton" the poet seemed to have forgotten his reader. In "East Coker" the person of the speaker dominates ("So here I am," "In my beginning"), but there is some sense of a reader ("As we grow older"). In "The Dry Salvages" and "Little Gidding" the first person singular pronouns disappear. All references are to *we* and *us*. The impact of this shift is conveyed in the awareness that "In my beginning" of "East Coker" has become "what we call the beginning" in "Little Gidding." The significance of this tonal shift would seem to be that the poet wants to suggest the possibility of every individual's realizing the essential experience which is the matter of the *Quartets*.

Part V opens by calling our attention to the accomplishment of "East Coker" where the speaker moved from thinking that his origins determined his destiny to the conclusion that his death is a new beginning. But his use of

> What we call a beginning is often the end
> And to make an end is to make a beginning,   (p. 144)

does not seem especially religious. It certainly refers to the end which is this section of the poem, and it likewise suggests that we never know when we are beginning or ending something. Eliot's chief analogue is once again literature, and the effect of the analogy is to underline the fact that he is concerned with the workings of the mind as it tries successively to express itself: "Every phrase/And every sentence that is right . . . Every phrase and every sentence is an end and a beginning." Then the faith implicit in the motto of Mary Queen of Scots becomes more pronounced:

> And any action
> Is a step to the block, to the fire, down the sea's throat
> Or to an illegible stone: and that is where we start.

The poet brings together death (Mary, Charles I, Hercules, the sons and husbands of "Dry Salvages") and his own pilgrimage to the graves and chapel of "Little Gidding." And in an abbreviated reference to Krishna he says that every action—whether it be the act of death or pilgrimage—equally leaves us with a new beginning.

Then come four cryptic lines in the poem:

> We die with the dying:
> See, they depart, and we go with them.
> We are born with the dead:
> See, they return, and bring us with them.

The lines are puzzling only because of the last line. How do the dead return? Through memory (the rose garden), imagination (the rustic dancers), apparitions (the dead master)? The lines are a gloss on Heraclitus—the four elements are now the living and the dead in a constant process of interrelation. Life and death, love and "temporal reversion," are equally momentary, two parts of a whole: "The moment of the rose and the moment of the yew tree/Are of equal duration." To understand this, to participate in it, one must perceive the meaning not "of one life only/But of many generations" (p. 133). We cannot comprehend time, we cannot redeem it, unless we can grasp its moments:

> A people without history
> Is not redeemed from time, for history is a pattern
> Of timeless moments.   (p. 144)

In tracing out the details of the speaker's reflections we may have left behind the qualities of character which helped to account for the precise interests and preoccupations that make up the speaker's thought. Yet the doubt and persistence, the passionate yet hesitant pursuit of the perfection of will for right action, seem almost to prescribe some such pattern as the "vision-lost-search-recovery" movement just elaborated.

The speaker's reflections in the *Four Quartets* have marked out a course which is an electric and poetic "Ascent to 'Little Gidding.'" The general movement is an approach to union with the Divine Logos ("a further union/A deeper communion," p. 129) by comprehending four views of the past. The eclecticism gives the reader private symbols of houses and places, the wisdom of east and west, and attempts to make some meaning out of the nightmare of history as well as the frightening encroachments of old age. The poetic nature of the meditation leaves the reader with a series of metaphors and images reconciling the enigma of man's wisdom and God's wisdom, human time and God's time. The most emphatic image reconciling these differences is the still point figure. The way men achieve this still point is explained as analogous to an Incarnational view of life.

The reflections in the *Quartets* are the speaker's fullest comprehension of the opening lines:

> Time present and time past
> Are both perhaps present in the future
> And time future contained in time past.   (p. 117)

The poem exists as a meditative dramatization of how a person who accepts the Incarnation feels about time. The abstract formulation of the opening lines was never repudiated, but it simply could not be held emotionally in the language first expressed. To express and to realize the full meaning of these lines the poet undertakes his journey to "Little Gidding"—both for himself and his reader. The passage through regret, humility, suffering, and prayer brings the poet and reader to view the opening conception in a total context. The poet at the end of the *Quartets* knows what to look for, and he can now see, or know, because of that. What he sees is what was always there, but now he looks at it with an understanding of what he seeks. Desire and knowledge, stillness and movement, suffering and love, "the fire and the rose" all are seen as part of one design. Looking will not now cease, it has only begun. But the speaker, and presumably the reader, now knows what to look for; he has moved through the illumination of time to the union in prayer with the Divine Logos.

Katharine Worth

Eliot and the Living Theater

I

No playwright of our time has been more difficult to "see" than Eliot. The poetry and the piety have worked a potent spell, obscuring both dramatic weaknesses and actual or potential strengths. The argument of this essay is that to be seen in perspective Eliot's plays must be seen in the context of the living theater, not as an extension of the poetry and the dramatic theory, nor as a special kind of activity called "religious drama."

We know that Eliot desperately wanted to elude the kind of audiences who attended his early plays expecting "to be patiently bored and to satisfy themselves with the feeling that they have done something meritorious."[1] His anxiety to make contact with "real" audiences was an important factor in the evolution of his post-war style. He put the poetry on a thin diet and overlaid his symbols with a conventionally seductive facade.

Yet the plays seem to keep their place in the not very jolly corner labeled "verse and religious drama." Is the reason for this simply their inadequacy as plays? Must they always be performed in what Ivor Brown jocularly called "the crypt of St. Eliot's" and have they no relevance to the development of the modern theater? Are they quite out of the main stream, as far out as the plays of Masefield, Drinkwater and Stephen Phillips are now seen to have been?

[1] T. S. Eliot, "Poetry and Drama," *PP*, p. 79.

From Eliot in Perspective, A Symposium, *ed. Graham Martin. Reprinted by permission of Macmillan London and Basingstoke. Copyright © 1970 by the Macmillan Co.*

I do not believe that we have to answer "yes" to these questions, though much of the existing criticism of the drama, no doubt against its intention, forces us to do so by emphasizing so heavily moral patterns, Christian solutions and thematic progressions. What in my view emerges as theatrically interesting, and what gives Eliot a place, however tentative, in the main stream, is his feeling for alienation and violence, his gift for suggesting metaphysical possibilities in the trivial or absurd and his exploration of new dramatic means for working upon the nerves and pulses of an audience.

Of course these potentialities are imperfectly realized. Again and again he seems to be on the verge of striking out an entirely new line, of creating, even, the modern theater. Then he abandons the promising experiment, conceals the real experience. *Sweeney Agonistes* must be one of the most exciting beginnings ever made by a poet turning towards the theater, a Yeatsian concept of total theater, full of primitive power. *The Family Reunion* showed that the impulse of the fragments could be sustained in a full-length piece and opened out still new vistas; even in *The Cocktail Party,* though not acknowledged for what it is, sounds the note of Beckett and Pinter; not irrelevantly, as M. C. Bradbrook has noted,[2] do the title and situation of the play bring into mind *The Birthday Party.*

What these experiments grew from, why they were not followed up and Eliot's dramatic powers fully realized, are the questions we might expect criticism to be asking. But, on the contrary, critics tend to accept the idea of painful self-improvement from *The Rock* to *The Cocktail Party* which Eliot offers in *Poetry and Drama.* Few would be found, of course, to place the last plays, *The Confidential Clerk* and *The Elder Statesman*, at the summit of his achievement. These are fairly generally admitted to show a falling away of power, though even here, to some minds, the edification in the subject-matter is more than compensation for thinness of texture.[3] And there will, no doubt, always be some for whom *Murder in the Cathedral* has no need to abide our questions: "Of the greatness of *Murder in the Cathedral*, there can be no doubt—it may even be the greatest religious play ever written—and the other plays will survive if only as parts of the unity of which it is the finest element."[4] But setting aside these acts of homage to the subject-matter it has still been common form for Eliot's own chart of

---

[2] M. C. Bradbrook, *English Dramatic Form* (1965), p. 173.
[3] C. H. Smith, *T. S. Eliot's Dramatic Theory and Practice* (1963), p. 214.
[4] D. E. Jones, *The Plays of T. S. Eliot* (1960), p. 215. The most thoroughly documented account of the plays: an indispensable work of reference.

his progress to be taken as a basis for study, for *The Cocktail Party* to be seen, as he presents it, as a dramatic advance upon *The Family Reunion,* and for *Sweeney Agonistes* to be totally ignored.

Eliot is, then, not without responsibility for a situation in which his real theatrical powers are not recognized. In small ways, too, he has encouraged an untheatrical view, by allowing recordings of the choruses detached from their dramatic context; indeed, by making them himself, in a voice admirably suited to *Four Quartets* but hardly likely to increase our belief in the real existence of the Women of Canterbury. The early publication of *Sweeney Agonistes* in *Collected Poems* (1936) and its subsequent omission from *Collected Plays* (1962) has also served to misdirect. Even critics such as Northrop Frye and G. S. Frazer here referred to this most exciting theatrical piece as a "poem."

Criticism of poetic drama in our time has often taken untheatrical directions for want of a theatrical context, but there is no need for this in Eliot's case. A wealth of theatrical material exists, from reviews and actors' accounts of their roles to records of the growth of the texts under the pressure of stage requirements.

Two kinds of interest attach to this material. It has, in the first place, the interest which first-hand accounts of plays in preparation and production must always have for students of drama, offering a perspective which can never be quite the same as that from the study.[5] In the second place, it raises questions about Eliot's special kind of relationship with the theater world. Some of those involved in production of his plays were deeply committed to the idea of a "religious drama"; their commentaries often combine shrewd stage judgments with a tendency, common in non-theatrical criticism, to look through what is there in the play to what ought to be there.

How important was the influence from within the theatrical milieu in turning Eliot towards the morality patterns of the late plays is, indeed, one of the as yet unanswerable questions with which future criticism must be concerned. It is already clear from E. Martin Browne's illuminating accounts of his share in the plays [especially from *The Making of a Play* (1966)] that his own influence was of the greatest importance. In giving Eliot much needed advice on stage necessity, he was also moving him towards a less ambiguous and equivocal expression of theme; suggesting such changes as the replacement of the word "daimon" by "guardian" in Edward's analysis of his own condition and

[5] K. Tynan, *Tynan on Theatre* (Penguin, 1964). Kenneth Tynan's reviews, for instance, call attention to the stage effectiveness of the "chilly scenes" and suggest new ways of looking at the plays.

requiring an exact account of Celia's fate, which Eliot, we are told, had in the first draft left "as vague as, at the end of *The Family Reunion*, he had at first left Harry's" (p. 22). Whether this last change really was an improvement is a question to which different answers have been and will be given, according to whether the play is seen as the Christian morality it purports to be, or as an abortive attempt at a less easily defined structure, in which the word "daimon" is in fact the right one.

The many critics, in and out of the theater, who are in sympathy with Eliot's doctrinal intentions, will hardly recognize the existence of such alternatives, or will at least have no hesitation in emphasizing the orthodox interpretation of any play under discussion. But even the criticism uncommitted to a religious viewpoint sometimes seems slightly out of focus with what is happening in the plays, perhaps because critical argument is so often conducted in a context composed almost exclusively of Eliot's own theory and practice. Much light has been thrown on the plays by studies of the relation of theory and practice and of the plays to the poems, of sources and meaning, ritual and symbolic patterns. Yet the separation of the play from the theatrical context has its dangers, not least the danger of over-interpretation. A critic, like C. H. Smith, who tells us that she is "not primarily concerned with an evaluation of Eliot's work by current theatrical standards," may have, and, indeed, has many valuable insights to offer about the ritualistic overtones, but she is also liable to move a long way from stage or any other kind of reality, as she does in her account of Harcourt Reilly: "Sir Henry's ritual identity is suggested by his continual drink of gin with a drop of water (he is adulterating his spiritual nature with a drop of water, representing time, flux, and humanity)."[6]

II

Eliot has, of course, invited symbol-hunting of the Thurberish kind by his ubiquitous dropping of clues, followed up by the answer in his next lecture.

The critical reception given to *Sweeney Agonistes* is a case in point. This piece has attracted much scholarly attention as a source of theme and symbol. But its stage inventiveness was scarcely given credit until the production of 1965 in the memorial program, "Homage to T. S. Eliot," at the Globe Theatre, with jazz accompaniment by John Dank-

[6] C. H. Smith, *Eliot's Dramatic Theory*, pp. ix, 179.

worth, Cleo Laine as Doris and Nicol Williamson as Sweeney. Audience and reviewers were astonished on this occasion by the force and freshness of the piece; far from seeming a precious literary experiment, it was felt to be as alive as the sculpture by Henry Moore which preceded it on the stage. To one reviewer it seemed "in the same class as the Berlin classics of Brecht and Weill," to another it "uncannily" foreshadowed the British *avant garde* drama of the fifties.[7]

Literary critics, on the other hand, have tended to see it as a dead end, an experiment of limited interest, or even as the wrong turning which it seems to Grover Smith ". . . the farcical music hall style, without any indication that Sweeney is deliberately talking down, is an improper vehicle for this serious theme."[8]

The selection of a "farcical music hall style" for the serious theme is in fact the best evidence of the acute theatrical sense with which Eliot was endowed at the start of his dramatic career. Nothing in his later development is more impressive than the instinct he showed then for recognizing potentialities in popular and vulgar forms. In the waifs and strays of *Sweeney Agonistes* he hit upon just those types, derived from music hall and minstrel show, which thirty years later, in *Waiting for Godot*, were to be seen as the seed around which a modern drama could crystallize.

Fascination with music hall, circus, revue, and the ritualistic interpretations of them offered by scholars like F. M. Cornford was of course a feature of *avant garde* movements in the 1920s. Paris was then, as later, a breeding-ground. e. e. cummings, another young American, like Eliot at home in literary Paris, produced his own highly original blend of ritual and burlesque, *Him*, in New York, only two years after Eliot's Aristophanic fragments had appeared in the *Criterion*, and Cocteau's voice was frequently heard in that journal, prophesying the future role of "le cirque, le music hall, le cinématographe." The ideas were in the air, but no one saw further into them than Eliot.

The ambiguity of his attitude towards the music hall experience largely accounts for the originality of the form he drew out of it. He was greatly struck by the possibilities it offered for a ritualistic drama: "Little Tich, George Robey, Nellie Wallace, Marie Lloyd . . . provide fragments of a possible English myth. They effect the Comic Purga-

[7] A recording of this production is available in "Homage to T. S. Eliot," produced by Vera Lindsay (E.M.I. Records). Reviews in the *Guardian* and *The Times*, 14 June 1965.

[8] Grover Smith, *T. S. Eliot's Poetry and Plays: a study in sources and meaning* (1956), p. 118.

tion."[9] These possibilities are no doubt uppermost in his mind when he emphasizes what might to most people seem the quality least character- istic of music hall, the "pure and undefiled detachment" which he found in performers of the supreme class. It sometimes seems that Eliot was attending the Islington Empire with a cold eye, seeing in the grotesqueness of some of the turns an approximation to that ideal, inhuman drama of masked beings which visited his imagination as it did that of Yeats.

Yet if we see for ourselves, even in the imperfect record of early film, a performance by one of Eliot's favorite artists, Little Tich, it becomes apparent that in stressing the detachment and impersonality of the great performers Eliot was making a profoundly imaginative judg- ment. It is easy enough now, after *Waiting for Godot* and *The Care- taker*, to see how the figure of Little Tich, a solitary, inscrutable dwarf, patiently manipulating his Brobdingnagian boots, was pointing the way for the modern theater. But in the 1920s it took an Eliot to see it, to recognize in Little Tich the qualities he found in Massine, of whom he said, "Massine, the most completely unhuman, impersonal, abstract, belongs to the future stage."[10]

Yet his awareness of the impersonal quality in the art of music hall did not prevent him from responding to its human warmth, as his loving essay in the first number of the *Criterion* on the occasion of Marie Lloyd's death shows very clearly. He admired the unself-consciousness, the proletarian vitality and, above all, the sense of human solidarity felt in the close collaboration between artist and audience. Some of this "normal" human warmth comes through in *Sweeney Agonistes*, giving the fragments a quality which none of the later plays capture, even when Eliot is trying hard for it. The unsentimental, matter-of-fact relationship between Doris and Dusty projects a real sense of human closeness, a closing of the ranks against Pereira and the other menacing facts of their existence.

The special quality of the piece, however, springs from the skillful turning of elements derived from a warm, popular art to effects of isolation and disorientation. It is an exercise in black comedy whose success depends upon the sustaining of the popular note just long enough for the distortion to register. Heavily syncopated rhythms suggest sexual excitement passing into a state of hysteria and spiritual panic. The jovial nightmare song from Gilbert and Sullivan takes a

[9] Cited in J. Isaacs, *An Assessment of Twentieth-Century Literature* (1951), p. 146.

[10] T. S. Eliot, "Dramatis Personae," *Criterion*, I (1923), iii, 305.

sickening lurch into real nightmare, conveying in musical terms the experience Sweeney cannot find words for, the swallowing up of the known by an unknown world:

> You dreamt you waked up at seven o'clock and it's
>   foggy and it's damp and it's dawn and it's dark
> And you wait for a knock and the turning of a lock
>   for you know the hangman's waiting for you.
> And perhaps you're alive
> And perhaps you're dead
> Hoo ha ha
> Hoo ha ha
> Hoo
> Hoo
> Hoo

This is "physical" theater, where the poetry combines with the actors' bodily movements to draw primitive responses from the audience. Eliot may have been encouraged in his experiment by seeing the performance of Yeats's *At the Hawk's Well* in Lady Cunard's drawing-room, to which Ezra Pound had taken him in 1916. Although he later dismissed the *Plays for Dancers* as more decorative than dramatic, he was at the time of that performance struck by a modern quality in Yeats which he had not perceived before. It took an acute sense of theatrical possibilities to recognize this "modernity" in *At the Hawk's Well*, with its legendary hero, hawk goddess for heroine, and choral interludes from a group of musicians on the stage. But Eliot may well have had in mind Yeats's use of drum, gong and zither when, in 1924, he outlined to Arnold Bennett a project for a drama of modern life, "perhaps with certain things in it accentuated by drum beats."[11]

In *Sweeney Agonistes* he catches the drum beat in the verse: it plays upon the nerves, assaults the audience physically, suggesting meanings below the line which can only be apprehended in the beat. The play offers an experience of almost total alienation. The borrowings from music hall "turns" like the soft-shoe number heighten the sense of isolation: as characters go into their routines, they convey the essential solitariness of the music-hall performer before he makes contact with his audience, an idea later to be taken up by John Osborne in *The Entertainer*. There is a sustained threat in the verse rhythms, balanced as they are, and as the Dankworth production well brought

---

[11] The relevant passage from *The Journals of Arnold Bennett* is quoted in Jones, *Plays of Eliot*, p. 27.

out, on the edge of a great jazz explosion, which powerfully suggests the emotional explosion to which the action must move. That this explosion was to take the form of murder, real or "acted out," is shown in early drafts of the play.[12]   As the action stands, all the detail points to a slow moving together of Doris, the predestined victim, who has already turned up the coffin card, and Sweeney, the man obsessed with the thought of violence:

> Any man has to, needs to, wants to
> Once in a lifetime, do a girl in.

A play about spiritual "lostness," expressed in the vocabulary of the jazz age, moving towards a symbolic act of violence, *Sweeney Agonistes*, even in its fragmentary state, was a very long step in a new theatrical direction. That it remained unfinished because, as Hugh Kenner says,[13]   "there was nowhere for it to go" has been disproved by the whole course of post-war theater. Eliot's abandonment of the fragments may have been due to something in the subject-matter which he was not yet able to get under artistic control, or it may have been, as C. H. Smith suggests, the result of his conversion and reception into the Church of England which followed shortly after the publication of the piece.

The effect of this change in his life on his dramatic writing was great and in some ways damaging. From *The Rock* onwards, much of his energy went into an effort to extend his range, so as to accommodate, within the drama of alienation natural to him, the opposite experience of communion. The strain involved in this attempt creates the "second voice," the voice of "myself addressing, even haranguing an audience," which dominates the choruses for *The Rock* and is strong in *Murder in the Cathedral.*

Religious influences may have been reinforced by the didactic drama of Auden and Isherwood, who, perhaps inspired by the printed version of *Sweeney Agonistes*, were pursuing the direction indicated in it during the years when *The Rock, Murder in the Cathedral* and *The Family Reunion* were being written. The Group Theater who produced their plays were dedicated to the exploration of popular techniques;

---

[12] A manuscript draft, reproduced in the program of "Homage to T. S. Eliot," has stage directions for the entry of Mrs. Porter after the chorus "The Terrors of the Night"; a debate with Sweeney; her murder and, finally, the "Return of Mrs. Porter."

[13] H. Kenner, *The Invisible Poet: T. S. Eliot* (1960), p. 186.

they envisaged a new drama, "analogous to modern musical comedy or the pre-medieval folk play" and in pursuit of this curious-sounding goal they explored the possibilities in dance, jazz effects and visual shock tactics such as masks.

"We should like less prancing and bad dancing" was Geoffrey Grigson's comment on the Group Theater style, a remark which perhaps Eliot might have endorsed if, as Professor Isaacs tells us,[14] he was "puzzled" by the production the theater gave *Sweeney Agonistes* in 1935. He may well have considered that the notion of putting his characters into full or half masks destroyed the delicate tension he had built up between a commonplace surface and a profoundly disturbing underpattern. Yet, in giving him a production of his play, and in drawing his attention to Auden and Isherwood in performance, the Group Theater were encouraging him to continue his exploration of the possibilities in revue techniques. Certainly, *Murder in the Cathedral* owes a good deal of its theatrical life to flamboyant changes of rhythm. Its contemporary political flavor, too, in the totalitarian apologetics of the Knights, seems to point to the engaged drama of Auden and Isherwood, as later *The Family Reunion* was to show some striking similarities to *The Ascent of F6*.

If there was then this influence operating in *Murder in the Cathedral*, it is not likely to have lessened Eliot's difficulties in dealing with ordinary people like the Women of Canterbury and showing them in a convincing human relationship with Becket, or, indeed, with anyone else in the play. The characteristic hero of Auden and Isherwood, in all his high-minded liberalism, has as little real contact with the "people" whose cause he espouses as has Ransom of *The Ascent of F6* with the suburban Mr. and Mrs. A, isolated in their stage boxes.

The isolation in that instance is delicate. But in *Murder in the Cathedral* the isolated elements are meant to coalesce, Chorus and Saint to come together in the redemption of one by the death of the other. That there has been an interior happening of this kind is declared poetically with such skill as almost to convince that it has happened dramatically too. But it has not. The Chorus are not involved in any human relationship with Becket real enough to move belief in his having power to affect their lives. They are only a collective voice, not living people with a stake in the action. Becket addresses them, typically from a physical height above them, in the pulpit, but hardly speaks to them. Whether his awareness of them affects his own inner develop-

---

[14] Isaacs, *An Assessment,* p. 147.

ment is extremely debatable. Production could certainly make it seem that when he has his moment of illumination—

> Now is my way clear, now is the meaning plain:
> Temptation shall not come in this kind again—

it comes to him through listening to the entreaties of the Chorus,

> O Thomas Archbishop, save us, save yourself
>   that we may be saved;
> Destroy yourself and we are destroyed.

But the recognition could with equal, if not greater theatrical plausibility, be shown as self-generated, coming out of the deep trance of self-communion in which Beckett is engaged for most of the play.

Eliot admitted to having difficulty in imagining the Chorus; it seems that he was able to imagine their thoughts, but not what they were actually doing, particularly at the crisis of the murder. If they are present at this event, it can only be as mute spectators, like the Priests who, as the director of the film version, George Hoellering, pointed out, "do not lift a finger to come to his aid."[15] No attempt is made to express their helplessness as a dramatic element, nor is any notice taken of Chorus and Priests by the Knights, who, after the murder, address the audience directly, giving them the orders which, if given to the Chorus would have helped to involve them as human beings in the situation: "I suggest that you now disperse quietly to your homes. Please be careful not to loiter in groups at street corners, and do nothing that might provoke any public outbreak."

The various changes made in the film version were in the first place a response to the demands of the different medium; the Knights could not address a cinema audience at such length, so they had to be shown speaking to a crowd outside the cathedral. But some of these changes would, as Hoellering suggested, improve stage versions too; he saw the need for "tightening" the action by integrating the Women of Canterbury more closely into it and for increasing credibility by some quite simple rearrangements such as the dismissal of the Priests to vespers before the murder. Eliot accepted these alterations as "improvements" in a statement of some ambiguity: the play worked in the Chapter House at Canterbury, he implies, because it was not really trying to be a

---

[15] T. S. Eliot and G. Hoellering, *The Film of Murder in the Cathedral* (1952), p. 10.

play there: the film version "made the meaning clearer, and in that way is nearer to what the play would have been, had it been written for the London theatre and by a dramatist of greater experience."[16]

In failing to come to life as a play about the interaction of people, *Murder in the Cathedral* fails to become the new kind of play Eliot's religious belief compelled him to attempt. It is weakest in those areas where themes of Christian redemption and brotherhood are being worked out, as the precarious attachment of the Chorus to the action shows. Where it has strength is in precisely that territory already shown in *Sweeney Agonistes* to be Eliot's own. The central action is, indeed, curiously close to the action outlined in the earlier play. Eliot himself points to its extreme simplicity: "A man comes home, foreseeing that he will be killed, and he is killed" (*PP*, p. 79). Anticipation of, and preparation for, an act of violence generates the greatest dramatic excitement felt anywhere in the piece. Becket is most fully realized as a human character when he is involved with the idea of death, in the preparatory clearing of conscience with the Four Tempters and in the murder scene itself, where the intimacy of his relationship with his murderers, usually stressed in production by the doubling of Tempters' and Knights' roles, goes far beyond the degree of intimacy he achieves with anyone else in the play.

The Chorus, too, finds the most dramatic of all its functions in winding up the suspense as the murder approaches, then releasing it in a great outburst which in its exultingly violent rhythms, conveys a Maenad-like impression of ecstasy in the sacrificial consummation:

> Clean the air! clean the sky!
> wash the wind! take the
> stone from the stone . . . Wash
> the stone, wash the bone . . .
> wash them wash them!

They may not be able to communicate as personalities, but they do, though with some monotony, convey a state of mind with which Eliot is, dramatically speaking, at home; a state of "panic and emptiness." "The sense of disgust in the chorus," says Stevie Smith, "is the most living thing out of all the play."[17] The word "living" is correct here;

[16] *Ibid.*, p. 13.

[17] This and the following comment on *Murder in the Cathedral* occur in Stevie Smith's essay "History or Poetic Drama?" in *T. S. Eliot: a symposium for his seventieth birthday*, ed. N. Braybrooke (1958), pp. 172-3.

their "disgust" grows out of the action, moves with it and is finally appeased in the ritual killing.

Fascination with violence as a cleansing, therapeutic process is strongly felt in *Murder in the Cathedral*. Virginia Woolf once said, "If you are anaemic as Tom is, there is a glory in blood"; without accepting her explanation of the cause, we may agree with her findings. There is a kind of glory in blood and violence in the plays, violence as a means of opening the doors of perception. Sudden death, often in shocking forms, is a recurring feature. The death of Celia was originally designed to be still more horrible than it appeared in the final version of *The Cocktail Party*,[18] and Stevie Smith is surely right in saying of *Murder in the Cathedral* that "the poetry mounts at each touch of pain." Eliot often seems to be on the verge of creating "the theatre of cruelty," but in the process gets into dramatic difficulties, since he is obliged by his didactic intentions to represent the cruelty as somehow leading to an advancement of human well-being all round. The unsatisfactory solutions of *The Family Reunion* and *The Cocktail Party* are the results of this internal contradiction.

Yet *The Family Reunion* (1939), despite its flawed ending, is more deeply satisfying than any other of the plays, more nearly a complete expression of his dramatic vision. Eliot's severe criticism of its stagecraft in *Poetry and Drama* is, in my view, one of his most misleading accounts of his own plays. He underestimates and even distorts, dismissing two of the most moving scenes, the "lyrical duets," between Harry and Mary and Harry and Agatha, as "remote from the necessity of the action" and giving up as a bad job the notion of representing in stage terms "those ill-fated figures, the Furies."

It would be interesting to know, and this is another of the questions with which future criticism might well be concerned, how far these curious judgments spring from experience of inadequate productions, how far from the need under which he seems to have labored, to apologize for, or turn away from, what is most alive and disturbing in his dramatic experiments. *The Family Reunion* has had some effective productions on stage and television since Eliot wrote so deprecatingly of it, notably, in my experience, by Michael Elliott, with a student cast, in 1966.[19] He successfully disregarded Eliot's injunction against making the Furies visible, contriving, with the aid of beautifully controlled

[18] See E. Martin Browne's account, in *The Making of a Play*, p. 22. See also his *The Making of T. S. Eliot's Plays* (1969).

[19] Michael Elliott's production was given on the floor of the rehearsal room at the Central School of Speech and Drama, Swiss Cottage, in 1966.

modulations of light into darkness, spectacular incarnations for them as towering black shapes, alarmingly materializing between the audience, who sat round a skeletal framework enclosing the haunted room, and the characters. Harry made his entrance through the room where the audience sat, pausing with them for a long look at the family exposed to view a few yards away in the lighted framework before stepping into it and exchanging the watcher's role for the actor's. By this simple arrangement, an experience which can seem private and obscure in the far distances of the picture-frame stage was brought nearer and made comprehensible. Indeed, Harry's awareness of the eyes upon the house seemed to an audience made conscious of themselves as watchers more natural than the blank incomprehension of the family when he tells them they are being watched:

> How can you sit in this blaze of light
>   for all the world to look at?
> If you knew how you looked, when I saw you
>   through the window!
> Do you like to be stared at by eyes through
>   a window?

This physical involvement of the audience in Harry's experience was completed when the Eumenides materialized between him and them, overlooking both, forcing them out of their safe role as watchers into the protagonist's situation of vulnerability to the inquisitorial eye. In appearance, these Furies were essentially shapeless, bundles of old clothes which might or might not contain life. They conveyed the fundamental ambiguity of Eliot's Furies, black and malign to view in the first shock of their appearance, yet perhaps to be seen differently, as soaring, upward-pointing beings. The question remained open: the movement toward an orthodox Christian solution at the end was not strong enough to obliterate the disturbing impression made by the strong physical impact of these Eumenides.

Imaginative staging of this kind makes it clear that in *The Family Reunion* Eliot had worked out a technique of special interest to the modern theater, a method of dealing with metaphysical questions in a drama of contemporary life. He was pointing in a direction later to be taken by Beckett and Pinter: *The Birthday Party* has some striking likenesses to both *The Family Reunion* and *The Cocktail Party,* while the symbolism of the spiritual eye connects Eliot's play in an interesting way with the spotlight in *Play* which indicates to its victims the possibility that they are being "seen." The claustrophobic Wishwood interior, menaced by mysterious visitants, has, indeed, become a theatrical commonplace of our time.

The maintenance of a degree of ambiguity is an important element in the success of the play. Some strain is put upon it by the orthodox turning given to Harry's "conversion" at the end. The faint suggestion of an emerging missionary motif strikes a discordant note which would have quite upset the dramatic balance had it been developed along the lines indicated to Michael Redgrave when he pressed Eliot for more definition in the ending: "Oh yes, I think he and the chauffeur go off and get jobs in the East End."[20]

If there is, as Eliot suggests, a "failure of adjustment between the Greek story and the modern situation," this is where it lies, not in the confrontation of the Oresteian Harry with his Furies, a situation well within his dramatic range. But *The Family Reunion* is more than the characteristic ghost-play; it is also, and uniquely in the dramatic canon, a deeply moving play about human relationships, not only in their aspects of bitterness and failure, which are well captured in other plays, but also in aspects of tenderness and real intimacy.

One main reason for the much fuller human quality of this play is Eliot's acknowledgment of imperfection in all the characters, including, and especially in, the spiritually sensitive. That he was not altogether in conscious control of the process is suggested by his dismay on discovering that Harry was "an insufferable prig." It is understandable that he, who criticized D. H. Lawrence's people for their "insensibility to ordinary social morality,"[21] should find the prominence of this trait in his own heroes an embarrassment. For their indifference to social morality is a striking feature of their behavior: in sexual matters especially, they are airily amoral. Even the gentle Celia feels no qualms of conscience over her adultery with Edward, while Agatha, an eminently ruthless being, glories in her special relation with Harry, described by Eliot himself as "ambiguous," which is the fruit of her liaison with his father.

The strength of *The Family Reunion* consists in the recognition of these ambiguities, the admission that there is a neurotic element in the spirituality of Harry and Agatha, that Amy's "human" criticism of them has validity. As a result, the spiritual climax, Harry's private illumination, becomes also a human climax, involving three people,

[20] Michael Redgrave's account of his conversations with Eliot is given in R. Findlater, *Michael Redgrave* (1956), pp. 49-50.

[21] *ASG*, p. 39. Lawrence's characters are said to be "unfurnished with even the most commonplace kind of conscience."

Harry, Agatha and Mary, in a delicate emotional consummation which depends for its effectiveness upon an awareness of them as deeply wounded, even crippled, human beings. That "crippled" is not too strong a term is indicated by Eliot's own account of his intentions.[22] Harry was meant to show "the attraction, half of a son and half of a lover, to Agatha, which she reciprocates in somewhat the same way," while in his relation with Mary he was to convey the "conflict inside him between . . . repulsion for Mary as a woman, and the attraction which the normal part of him that is left, feels toward her personally for the first time."

In the face of such emotional difficulties, the achievement of even a transient human contact should be felt as a touching achievement, as indeed it was in Michael Elliott's production, which avoided the trance-like, inhuman effect often seen in performance, by moving the characters towards each other as the verse mounted to its climax. The embrace in which they met, sexless, yet touched with sexual tenderness, delicately suggested a real human communion at some deep level of being. Far from being undramatic, "beyond character," as Eliot puts it, these "duets," in which poetic rhythm and imagery are put to intensely theatrical use, take us deep into character, communicating below the level of conscious thought, offering, indeed, a means to the only kind of communication in which the modern theater really believes.

III

This study has been chiefly concerned with the earlier plays, in an attempt to show Eliot's range, theatrical originality and real achievement.

To do any sort of justice to the later plays would require a separate study, but one aspect of them may, perhaps, reasonably be considered in brief space, the comic or farcical forms in which they are cast.

Eliot's adoption of a Coward-Wilde formula has sometimes been thought the cause of the drying-up process in these plays, a sacrifice, for the sake of acquiring an audience, to the gods of the West End theater, and a useless sacrifice, since the formula had already lost its theatrical vitality. It seems unlikely that his acute sense of the contemporary had so completely deserted him. The choice of farce is, rather, a

---

[22] The relevant passage is quoted in F. O. Matthiessen, *The Achievement of T. S. Eliot* (1935), pp. 167-8.

proof of his continuing sensitivity to formal necessities. It offered him the withdrawal he needed to make, for whatever reason, from the emotional intensity of earlier work. That it was the right form, in offering a measure of control over the sentimental tendencies of the later phase, may be seen by comparing *The Confidential Clerk* with *The Elder Statesman*, a neo-Ibsenite structure in which sentimentality is allowed full play.

Coward's comedy offered patterns of separation and estrangement which could easily be adapted to Eliot's purposes. Coward too has his "elect" and his "damned"; on one side of the deep divide are the "ordinary moral, high-thinking citizens," on the other, the amoral but honest and therefore more admirable Bohemians.[23]

This Calvinistic world, in which the elect remain the elect, no matter what they do, offered Eliot an escape from the need which had always proved so troublesome to him of translating spiritual experiences into terms of ordinary social morality. He takes advantage of this new freedom in *The Confidential Clerk* to explore, through the fantastically amoral situations of the play, various kinds of ambiguity. The skill with which the ambiguity is sustained, so that even after the oracular pronouncements of Mrs. Guzzard, the question of Colby's identity remains central, is something new in Eliot's drama. It shows him still very much in the main stream, offering an original means for handling themes which were to preoccupy the Pirandello-conscious theater of the mid-century.

The Cocktail Party also has this kind of relevance. It hints the possibility of a "black" theater coming out of the Coward formula. One of the most impressive features of the play is the extraction of grim significance from the fussy detail, the seemingly empty chatter, the farcical poppings in and out of the party scene in the first act. The effect of a remorseless machine at work is very well done. The frivolous, banal context brings out the chilling quality in lines like Julia's "I like to manage the machine myself," and heightens the horror of the last act in which Reilly smoothly describes his vision of poor, murdered Celia, and Alex makes his grotesque jokes about monkeys and mutilated Christians.

[23] Gilda, in *Design for Living,* when she apologizes to her deceived husband, not for deceiving but for "using" him—"I've made use of you, Ernest. I'm ashamed of that"—seems to point to Celia making her similar apology to Edward. Other echoes abound, Eliot, in customary sly style, drawing attention to their source in his choice of Teddington, Coward's birthplace, as the home of Mrs. Guzzard, and the place where the babies are hopelessly mixed up.

The Cocktail Party convinces when it is being a play about hell, the characteristic hell of Eliot's drama, an unhappy marriage. It was as such a play that it first came into his mind.[24] When contemplating the Alcestis legend and wondering what kind of life would have been possible for Admetus and Alcestis after her return from the "death" wished upon her by her husband, he was thinking along lines which make fully explicable in formal terms his choice of the Coward convention for his Alcestis play. His view of the story and its "happy" ending was more deeply skeptical even than Euripides', who provided his dramatic model. Where the Euripidean version, in reducing the legend to unheroic proportions, had allowed Alcestis at least some heroic virtue, Eliot made her and her Admetus equal in selfishness. He removed the selfless qualities of her classical prototype from the married woman, Lavinia, to give them to the unmarried Celia, the woman who will have no truck with domesticity. This pointed distinction, and the sardonic representation of married domesticity as a long waiting for a cocktail party, have the effect of going beyond criticism of individual characters, to raise doubt about the viability of marriage as a way of life. Despite the formal contradiction of the proposition in the last act, it is nevertheless this doubt, so well established in stage terms, which emerges as a major theme of the play.

To make central a subject clearly so painful to him, Eliot probably needed the distancing devices of artificial comedy. Coward's frivolous anti-marriage plays offered suitably stylized expression. Eliot takes over their conventional assumptions—marriage is a joke and adultery a game—and sets out to show, not that Coward is wrong, but that the joke is a very black one, the game a sour business. The scenes of recrimination between Edward and Lavinia are done with a bitter intensity recalling the Strindbergian dance of death. As in Strindbergian drama, too, the onus is placed rather more upon the wife than the husband. Both are involved in extra-marital affairs—and seldom in stage history can there have been drearier ones—but Edward's situation allows him opportunities which are denied Lavinia for showing some emotional complexity. He is permitted to make a bid for sympathy in his account of his wretchedness:

[24] In an interview with Donald Hall, printed in the *Paris Review*, XXI (Spring/-Summer, 1959), pp. 48-70, Eliot says of Lavinia and Edward: "Those two people were the centre of the thing when I started and the other characters only developed out of it." This interview is reprinted in *Writers at Work: The Paris Review Interviews*, Second Series (1963), pp. 77-94.

> What is hell? Hell is oneself,
> Hell is alone, the other figures in it
> Merely projections.

Lavinia is more firmly entrenched in the cool, passionless Coward world, where "love" is a word used with conscious mockery: "I love you. You love me. You love Otto. I love Otto. Otto loves me. There now! Start to unravel from there!"

"Unravelling," for Coward a purely comic process, turns in Eliot's hands into the unwinding of a labyrinthine thread leading through dark places. The thread is firmly held by the Guardians, that menacing trio of watchers and manipulators, through whom he gets his blackest comic effects. They begin by seeming feeble imitations of lovable eccentrics in the Coward-Wilde tradition, a rather tame joke. But the joke is on the audience. The imitation is not meant to convince, only to sketch a half-mask, which draws attention to the real faces underneath, faces of alarming power. Again, as in *The Family Reunion,* the force controlling the action, whose agent the Guardians are, is represented by a watchful eye; in this play it has a disquieting likeness to the omnipresent Orwellian eye which haunts the modern mind. The likeness is strengthened by the image of the single eye shared by three, an image pointing to the legend of the Gorgon and her petrifying stare. Whether or not the audience catch such allusions, they cannot miss the oppressive watchfulness of the Guardians, the ostentatious contriving of exits and entrances to ensure that an eye is being kept on the movements of the "patients." Nor, one would think, can they miss a suggestion of gratuitous cruelty in Celia's death, the account of which is so loosely tacked on to the main action that it amounts, as Eliot suspected, to no more than an epilogue, in which form, in fact, he had originally written it.

What makes *The Cocktail Party* finally unsatisfactory is not of course the unpleasantness of its characters, nor the blackness of its jokes, but the insistence that all this is not so, that it is a play about heaven as well as about hell. Here, of course, the Coward formula works against Eliot's intention, rather as do the Wilde mannerisms against the pious conclusion of *The Confidential Clerk.* For though the formula allows for a good deal of oddity—it can accommodate an unprofessional psychiatrist, a son choosing his parents from a plethora of candidates, even a "suburban Pallas Athene,"[25] granting wishes all round—what it

[25] See Alison Leggatt's "A Postscript from Mrs. Chamberlayne and Mrs. Guzzard," in Braybrooke's *Symposium*, pp. 79-80.

does not allow are situations of domestic snugness and sweetness, such as *The Cocktail Party* offers. Ideas of conversion and reform are alien to it; when Eggerson predicts a future for Colby as a chapel organist reading for orders the effect is as grotesque as though *Design for Living* were to end with Gilda taking up welfare work.

In selecting a form giving splendid opportunities for exploring conditions of alienation but none at all for solution in terms of "ordinary, social morality," Eliot followed his theatrical instinct, though only by making things difficult for himself as a moralist. It has been the object of this study to suggest how strong that theatrical instinct was, however fitfully it worked. Future criticism, it may be hoped, will explore more thoroughly in theatrical directions, finding answers to some of the perplexing questions raised by the many changes of Eliot's dramatic style.

The plays can stand such scrutiny; uneven, flawed, though they may be, they remain an achievement of great interest, not merely to admirers of Eliot the poet, but to lovers of the living theater, and it is in the context of the living theater that the kind of dramatic interest they have shows most clearly.

Helen Gardner

T. S. Eliot

It is perhaps too early for anyone to attempt an assessment of the achievement of T. S. Eliot as poet, critic, and man of letters. His correspondence has not been published; there seems little prospect of an authoritative biography; and the discovery of the supposedly lost manuscript of *The Waste Land*, the publication of extensive quotations from the drafts of the plays, and the knowledge that comparable material exists for the study of the growth of *Four Quartets*[1] make this an unpropitious moment for the discussion of Eliot as an artist. We need time to come to terms with this new image of a fluent writer who pared down his first drafts and learned what he had to say in process of saying it. If it is said that all this missing and new information is strictly irrelevant to discussion of the value of Eliot's poetry and criticism, the pure critic, if such a creature can be said to exist, is uneasily aware that it is difficult at the moment to get Eliot in focus. He is suffering the fate that overtakes every famous writer on death: a reaction that has in it a good deal of malice, like the malice of schoolboys when the master

All quotations from Eliot's verse are from *Collected Poems 1909-1962* (New York, 1963), and are reprinted here by permission of Harcourt Brace Jovanovich, Inc.

I have to thank the editor of the *New Statesman* for permission to print in a revised and expanded form material that appeared in that journal on 28 November 1969.

[1] At the invitation of Mrs. Eliot I am at present working on a book on the composition of *Four Quartets*.

has just left the room. What truth there is in the anti-Eliot movement will have to be digested in time. At the moment he is neither a living presence nor a historic figure. Yet, even if the time for a reassessment had come, I could not attempt it. His poetry is too much a part of my own experience, from the time when, as an undergraduate, I read *The Waste Land*, and knew "Prufrock" and the quatrain poems by heart, to the moment when, in the dreary spring of 1940, I read "East Coker" on its appearance in the *New English Weekly*, and realized that a poet I had rather written off in the political thirties was still the poet, above all others then writing, who could make me feel "Yes, this is where I am." A prime source of Eliot's power is that again and again he touches the raw nerve of experience, experience that is often painful and disturbing but which is transformed by his expression of it into something that can be contemplated and understood. His poetry is a poetry that "questions the distempered part" and in doing so resolves, or at least moves towards resolving, enigmas. For me it has worn well, and I think it always will.

It has to be conceded that Eliot's poetry appears to have little influence at present, and that his plays, far from having inaugurated a new era of poetic drama, have been made to appear old-fashioned by the arrival of the "new" drama of the fifties. Only the fragmentary *Sweeney Agonistes* seems "modern" today; it might, as has justly been said, have very well been called "Waiting for Pereira."[2] His critical revaluations have been revalued, many by himself, and the questions his criticism was most concerned with are not at the center of critical concern today. One no longer expects to find critics taking one of Eliot's sentences or phrases as almost a sacred text to be expounded or glossed. The sociological writings on which he spent so much time and thought are largely ignored. Yet I cannot change my sights and try to look at Eliot from some supposed standpoint of the seventies. He remains the poet who made sense to me of my own experience of life and of the age I lived in. I do not mean by this that I accepted all his views, religious, political, or literary. I mean that, of all the poets writing in the period between the two wars, he most seriously and persistently took upon himself the burden of his time, and labored to express his sense of it as exactly and truthfully as he could. He submitted himself to experience, including the experience of growing old, and attempted to discover in personal distress and world catastrophe a way of life. His career was a long quest of the mind and spirit to

[2] See William V. Spanos, " 'Wanna Go Home, Baby?': *Sweeney Agonistes* as Drama of the Absurd," *PMLA*, 85 (January, 1970), pp. 8-20.

discover a pattern in living that would give unity and meaning to the flux of feelings, events, and experiences that make up the disorder of daily life. He did not rest content with the expression of personal distress or disgust, or with recording fleeting moments of delight, but attempted to discover the meaning of his experience, and in so doing discovered grounds for faith and hope. Where others took refuge in fables and myths, he went deeper and deeper into history.

In so doing he was extending to the art of living his convictions about the art of poetry. From the beginning Eliot realized that no poet starts from scratch. Whether he is aware of it or not, the material of his art—words and their meanings, rhythms of speech and those artificial arrangements of natural rhythms we call meters—and the techniques of his art are things he has not made but inherits; and what he in turn makes of them he does not make for himself alone or for his generation alone. Eliot saw very early as a poet what came to be the great theme of his later poetry: the involvement of past and future in the present. The famous essay on "Tradition and the Individual Talent" saw every true poet as altering the map of poetry, changing our view of what went before and creating conditions for what is to come after. In his later life and in his later poetry Eliot viewed the life of individual man and the life of mankind in the same way. Nobody can now miss in the early poetry the pressure of a distress that can only be called religious. There hangs over it an "overwhelming question" that Prufrock dare not even phrase as he thinks of

> Streets that follow like a tedious argument
> Of insidious intent
> To lead you to an overwhelming question . . .
> Oh, do not ask, "What is it?"
> Let us go and make our visit.

The Waste Land ends with longing for the rain to fall, with the invitation to "The awful daring of a moment's surrender," with the dream that the key that turned in the lock might turn again—that there might be a release from the prison of the self—with the memory of controlling a boat, and the hint that, in obedience to "controlling hands," the heart would respond as gaily as a boat. In the parodic wit of "The Hippopotamus," and the irony of "Mr. Eliot's Sunday Morning Service"—which plays as much over the priggish Mr. Eliot as over the polyphiloprogenitive "sutlers of the Lord" and their spotty young, whom he views with such distaste—religious satire springs from religious need. The poet who deliberately made himself a poet, by submission to the tradition of European poetry, submitted himself in the same way to the religious tradition of Europe. If there were any answer for him to the overwhelming question, it was to be looked for where others had found it through the centuries: the religious man must go to school to the saints as the poet must to the poets. As the poet learned his individual craft from the masters of the past, so the man found his individual way of life within the communion of the church of the country he had settled in, the Church of England. The poet accepted for transformation into his unique idiom the idiom of his own day, believing that the developments of a language in "vocabulary, in syntax, pronunciation and intonation—must be accepted by the poet and made the best of."[3] In the same way, he "made the best of" the church of his time and place. The leader of the modern movement, which was paradoxically an attempt to recover the values of the past in the present, did not change course when he accepted baptism and confirmation.

The rapidity with which Eliot established himself as leader of the modern movement is remarkable. It is possible that but for the outbreak of war, which caught him in Europe, he would have returned to Harvard in 1914, submitted his doctoral thesis on F. H. Bradley, and accepted the position waiting for him in the Harvard department of philosophy. Instead he went to Oxford, fell in love and married, and decided his vocation was poetry. In the following year he met Ezra Pound in London and showed him the poems he had written while at Harvard and in Paris. Pound, with that passion for good letters and that generosity that makes one forgive his follies and sins, recognized at once the brilliant originality of "Prufrock" and devoted his energies to the building of Eliot's reputation. *Prufrock and Other Observations*, a drab little volume of forty pages priced at one shilling, was published in June 1917. Five hundred copies were printed and the edition took four years to sell out. After a spell of schoolmastering, Eliot found employment at a bank and in his evenings lectured to adult education classes, while writing for Middleton Murry's *Athenaeum* the famous essays he collected in 1920 under the enigmatic title *The Sacred Wood*. It was a hard life, made harder by his wife's ill health and nervous instability. Two years later, in 1922, he became editor of a newly founded journal, the *Criterion*, whose first number contained *The Waste Land*.

With publication of *The Waste Land* Eliot became at once *the* modern poet, idolized by some, dismissed and derided by others; but

---

[3] "The Music of Poetry," *On Poets and Poetry* (1957), p. 37.

recognized by admirers and detractors alike as having made a decisive break with the late Romantic tradition. His admirers saluted him as an innovator comparable to Dryden, who revolted against the decadent metaphysical tradition, and to Wordsworth, who broke with decadent neoclassicism; his detractors saw him as a pretentious seeker after novelty and a literary Bolshevik. From publication of *The Waste Land* Eliot dominated the literary scene in England and indeed, to some extent, in the world. He is one of the few English poets who have won a continental reputation in their lifetime. His companions are Byron and Oscar Wilde, who both had the advantage of scandal to help them. Eliot won his world reputation in spite of the handicap of his extreme respectability. He was not only respectable in old age, when he became a grand old man of letters. The author of *The Waste Land* was a bank clerk and looked like one, with his stiff white collar, bowler hat, well-rolled umbrella, and exquisite formal manners. The idol of the avant-garde had no touch of the Bohemian in his appearance; he left to Ezra Pound such flourishes as a Texan sombrero and earrings. Although the poets of today do not acknowledge Eliot as their master, and many of the younger critics are occupied in taking him down several pegs, I do not believe that my generation was wrong to see him as a master and think that even those who repudiate his influence and dislike his poetry have inherited freedoms that he won. I believe the literary historians of the future, however they rank Eliot among the English poets, will have to speak of the years between the two wars as "The Age of Eliot."

It was not only as a poet that he was at the center. He followed up the essays in *The Sacred Wood* with a series of essays, many originally written as full-page reviews and articles for the *Times Literary Supplement*. In these he boldly redrew the map of English literary history, exalting Donne and the metaphysicals, "dislodging" Milton from his pre-eminence, paying homage to John Dryden, reviving the Jacobean dramatists, rejecting Shelley as incomprehensible and Tennyson and Browning as "ruminators." These essays were remarkable for other things beside immensely influential revaluations, many of which Eliot, to the dismay of some of his admirers and followers, subsequently "revalued." There was first their extraordinarily confident tone: a tone of authority. There was also the pertinacity with which they assaulted certain fundamental critical problems concerning the nature of poetry. They raise fundamental questions, questions that are not capable of receiving permanently satisfying answers but which have to be asked again and again: such questions as the nature of a poet's beliefs qua poet. Last, and perhaps most striking, was the critic's marvelous gift for quotation, the product of wide reading combined with a wonderfully sensitive ear.

Then again, as editor of the *Criterion* from 1922 to 1939, Eliot carried on, or revived, the tradition of the Victorian man of letters as critic of society. In the preface to the second edition of *The Sacred Wood* in 1928 he said that, when he wrote the essays he had collected in the first edition in 1920, he was concerned with the "integrity of poetry": that when we are considering poetry "we must consider it primarily as poetry and not another thing"—but that now he had passed on to another problem, "the relation of poetry to the spiritual and social life of its time and other times." This is very apparent in the essays he wrote and the lectures he gave in the twenties: in the famous discussion of the "dissociation of sensibility" supposed to have taken place in the late seventeenth century, and in the discussion of Shakespeare and Dante in the lecture on "Shakespeare and the Stoicism of Seneca," where the poet is virtually reduced to a mere mouthpiece for the ideas of his age. The *Criterion*, from the beginning, aimed at being more than a literary magazine. It was a review in the old-fashioned sense, an organ of opinion; and Eliot's long editorials were more concerned with cultural and social than with purely literary issues. He was here the heir of Coleridge and Arnold as a critic of industrial democracy. His position has, I think, been misunderstood and the range of his thought undervalued. He has been unjustly accused of sympathy with fascism because of his sympathy with certain French thinkers, notably Maurras, whose ideas contributed to fascist ideology. It would be juster to say that he was troubled by the problems for which fascism provided a false solution. He was primarily concerned with the preservation of human values, intellectual, cultural, and spiritual, in a society in which the human scale was disappearing. As was natural in a poet who wrote with such power on the terrible loneliness of great cities, who had "watched the smoke that rises from the pipes/Of lonely men in shirt-sleeves, leaning out of windows," who saw the crowd of automatons flowing over London Bridge to work, "And each man fixed his eyes before his feet," who was haunted at the thought that "Weeping, weeping multitudes/Droop in a thousand A.B.C.'s" and noted the "strained time-ridden faces" in the London tube, he feared and dreaded the morbid growth of great urban conglomerations, or "conurbations"—places where no man knows his neighbor and local pride, patriotism, and affections can find no soil to grow in. In these vast ant-heaps, replacing towns and cities of men, what is the role of the intellectual or the artist? What place has an artist in an industrial society, organized to make money, or in a society organized to secure the material well-being of its members? The question became linked in Eliot's mind with the question of the role of a church in secular society. None of the problems, religious, cultural, social, educational, which Eliot discussed in his editorials, and in books such as *The Idea of a Christian Society*, has been solved; but he did not attempt to evade them by nostalgic longing for an earlier age, a rural or aristocratic society gone forever. He did not "ring the bell backward" or "follow an antique drum." His concern was deep and serious, and it was a concern with the fundamental problem of the quality of life. It flowed into his later poetry and is one of the strands in the web of *Four Quartets.*

Lastly, as the director of Faber and Faber for forty years, from 1925 to his death, Eliot exercised with great discrimination and generosity the role of patron to the next generation of poets. Many of them held religious and political views far from his own; but to them he was universally known as "Uncle Tom," and the rather cramped little office upstairs which he inhabited at Fabers was the mecca of young poets in the thirties. The care and pains he took in criticizing poetry that was sent to him appear in the recently published letters to Keith Douglas,[4] a foretaste of what his published correspondence will show.

The first essay in *The Sacred Wood*, "The Perfect Critic," originally published in the *Athenaeum* in 1920, bore as a motto a text from Remy de Gourmont: "Eriger en lois ses impressions personelles, c'est le grand effort d'un homme s'il est sincère." It is an appropriate motto for Eliot's lifelong "wrestle with words and meanings" or, to use the words of Heraclitus which he set above "Burnt Norton," his effort not to rest in a wisdom of his own but to arrive at the logos common to all. His work is dominated by the desire to achieve "sincerity" in de Gourmont's sense, or, in his own words, "a condition of complete simplicity." It may seem paradoxical to speak of sincerity in characterizing the work of a poet so lacking in spontaneity, who has been dubbed the Invisible Poet, whose nickname was Possum, and who, as much when he was the idol of the avant-garde as when he was the distinguished elder statesman of the literary world, preserved so impeccably discreet a demeanor, displaying what I. A. Richards has described as a "formality, a precision, a concern for standards in dress and deportment, a kind of consciousness of conduct" which had about it "the ghostly flavour of irony . . . as though he were preparing a parody."[5] It may seem even

---

[4] *Times Literary Supplement*, 2 July 1970.
[5] "On T. S. E.," *Sewanee Review* (January-March, 1966), 26.

stranger to speak of complete simplicity as the aim of a poet whose
notorious obscurity has given occupation to whole tribes of scholiasts
offering conflicting guidance on the identity of Pipit,[6] the number of
persons involved in the drama of "Sweeney Among the Nightingales,"
the symbolism of the rose-garden, and the allegorical significance of
Mrs. Guzzard. But Eliot's personal reserve, his "deliberate disguises,"
the fence he set about his private life and most intimate feelings, were
necessary defenses for a poet aiming at truth more profound than mere
frankness offers, to be won by the disciplining of the feelings and the
submission of immediate impressions to other impressions to discover
their meaning through experience and the power of memory. And the
simplicity he aimed at was a simplicity "costing not less than everything," to be arrived at by the absorption of disparate and conflicting
experiences, not by a simplification.

   This way of thinking about the meaning of words is something that
Eliot both as a poet and a critic forces on his readers. "Trying to learn
to use words" was his own description of his occupation *entre deux
guerres*. He taught a whole generation a new awareness of language as
the material of the poet's art and trained his readers to read the poetry
of the past with a new alertness, diverting us from hasty and ill-con-
sidered raids on a poet's "thought" or a poem's "meaning" to the
gradual absorption of it by concentration on the language embodying
it. Pound, who divided the art of poetry into the use of words to evoke
visual phenomena, the use of words to register or suggest auditory
phenomena, and "a play or dance among the concomitant meanings,
customs, usages and implied contexts of the words themselves,"
thought that he exceeded Eliot in the second but that Eliot surpassed
him in the third. The huge bulk of Eliot criticism and the concentration
on the exegesis of his thought and symbolism is in danger of depriving a
new generation of readers of the profound poetic pleasure that Eliot's
earlier poetry offered to my generation. We delighted in such witty
dandyisms as "Reorganised upon the floor," and the contrast of a stale
pietism with modish jargon in "Flesh and blood is weak and frail,/
Susceptible to nervous shock"; we were moved by, and paused on, the
unexpectedly cold word "cogitations" at the close of "La Figlia che
Piange," were haunted by the "insidious intent" of the streets in
"Prufrock" and the "handful" of dust in *The Waste Land*. Striking
felicities are much rarer in the later poetry, though it can still astonish
and arrest us on a word—the "*disconsolate* chimera," the "*oppression*

---

[6] In a letter to me Eliot wrote that he thought the discussion in *Essays in
Criticism* on the identity of Pipit was "the nadir" in criticism of his poetry.

of the *silent* fog," the "parched *eviscerate* soil," a word that came late in the writing—but Eliot came to feel that poetry demanded a more "severe keeping," aimed at the ideal he expressed in the final section of "Little Gidding." He outgrew the virtuoso brilliance of his earlier poetry, where meaning concentrated itself in the image and developed, beyond symbolist theory, a style that was not afraid of statement. But the later poetry, though it develops from the earlier, is not either an improvement on it or a falling-off. The earlier has its own perfection. Today we need to read it for its own sake and less with Eliot's later poetry in mind, to pay more attention to its surface and less to fishing in its depths.

It is a poetry of the twenties, and many of its allusions, once commonplaces, now need elucidation. I found recently that it was necessary to explain to the young in the sixties what a "cooking egg" is. But I cannot believe that they will be helped to read the poem with this title by the suggestion that the name "Pipit" may carry a "learned and obscure 'egg' joke." "Pipi," one is informed in a recent *Student's Guide* "is the Greek misrendering of the Hebrew *Yahweh*, regarded by the occultists as a word of power: written on a shelled hard-boiled egg, it is said to open the heart to wisdom."

Such a note seems unlikely to open anybody's heart or mind to whatever wisdom is contained in this poem, and likely to militate against response to the wit and the sadness and the humanity of a poem which, trivial though it may seem, and even flippant, revolves around a permanently recurring mood of distress: "Is this really all that being 'grown-up' has to offer?" Having myself contributed to the mountains of commentary heaped on Eliot's poetry, I am not in a position to cast stones; and Eliot himself set us all a bad example, as he later ruefully owned, when at his New York publisher's request he eked out the scanty number of pages of *The Waste Land* by the addition of some unhelpful and perfunctory notes and "sent inquirers off on a wild-goose chase after Tarot cards and the Holy Grail." But at the moment we need less explication of the earlier poetry and to recover appreciation of its highly original, indeed unique, combination of a melancholy, even a depressing, subject matter with intellectual high spirits. Its true seriousness is destroyed by too solemn an approach. Its author, writing in 1928, defined poetry as "a superior amusement," adding that this was not a true definition, but that "if you call it anything else you are likely to call it something still more false."[7]

What persisted in Eliot was his devotion to his vocation as a poet,

[7] Preface to the second edition of *The Sacred Wood*.

which appears as a ceaseless process of experiment, a kind of sacred discontent with what had been achieved. He wrestled all his life with the material of his art, words and meanings, attempting to be as truthful as he could. It is a long way from "Portrait of a Lady," his first fully achieved poem, to "Little Gidding," his last. Both are in their way masterpieces of art, absolutely assured, with no uncertainty or weakness in diction or style. They are fully realized as poems. The attitudes are very different, in the one youthful and dandified, in the other mature; the first is semidramatic, the second is meditative, philosophic, and didactic. The technique in both is fully adequate to the author's purpose; the diction has the same blend of an apparent naturalness and ease with fastidious exactness. In each poem Eliot seems to have said exactly what he had to say at the time and no more. Each respects its own limits.

Unlike many poets, Eliot did not repeat his successes. He is the opposite of a writer who, after a period of experiment, finds his style and then goes on turning out competent repeats. The two early Jamesian monologues would, one feels, with any other writer have been only the first of a long series. He turned from them to the evocative "Preludes" and "Rhapsody on a Windy Night," and then from fluid free verse to the diamond-hard quatrain poems. The mythical monologue "Gerontion" in Jacobean blank verse led to the inspired ventriloquism of *The Waste Land*, with its dramatic "many voices." From this he moved to the opposite extreme of "The Hollow Men," a ghostly poem, stripped down to images without connexion, in lines that extend themselves into silences. From the inarticulacy of "The Hollow Men" he moved to the intensely personal, loose, relaxed, meditative style of *Ash-Wednesday*. None of these provided a style to rest in, or a formula for a poem. One might say that for longer poems the five-part structure of *The Waste Land* with its lyric fourth section, achieved by Pound's ruthless surgery, provided a model for *Four Quartets*; but the verse and method of the later poems are so different that it seems mere pedantry to point out that their ground plan is the plan of *The Waste Land*.

Each new poem or group of poems was "a wholly new start," or "a fresh beginning," a "raid on the inarticulate" from a different point of attack and employing new tactics. From "The Hollow Men" onwards each new venture was greeted with dismay by many of the most fervent admirers of the poem it succeeded. (One sometimes wonders how Eliot had the heart to go on in face of the groans of disappointment at his failure to continue doing the same thing.) Having written a poem, he seems to have felt that he had done with it, made it as good as he could, got it out of his system. He notoriously refused to discuss or comment on his poetry, and though he showed much more willingness to discuss his plays it was mainly their technical aspect he commented on. He declared more than once that a poem meant what the reader made of it. This was not affectation, but the way in which a humble and modest man confessed his belief in poetic inspiration. He neither suppressed nor rewrote his earlier poetry. Other poets in this century, notably Yeats and Auden, revised their early work, Yeats from dissatisfaction with his earlier style, Auden for more complicated reasons; and each new edition of Graves's *Collected Poems*, while it adds new poems, omits old. One poem that Eliot sent to press he withdrew at the proof stage, economically using some lines from it in *The Waste Land*. One published poem he did not reprint: "Ode" in the 1920 volume. Apart from this, each new volume of poems prints the earlier volumes with only minor revisions of style and corrections of misprints and punctuation. Eliot seems to have felt no urge to go back on what he had written.

Now that the early notebook and the original drafts of *The Waste Land* have turned up and large portions of the drafts of the plays are available, the notion of Eliot as a costive writer painfully squeezing out a few lines of verse is shown to be false. He wrote fluently; but he published little. He wove whole yards of cloth; out of it he cut and made up his poem. Having done so he took a remarkably objective view of it, concentrating on the "making," willingly entertaining criticism and suggestions. He thought of poetry as an art and not as a means of self-expression, and of the poet as a "maker" of a poem, not the giver of a personal testimony beyond criticism. It has long been known that Pound radically criticized *The Waste Land*, advising extensive cutting but strongly urging that the beautiful lyric on Phlebas the Phoenician, which Eliot wanted to drop, be kept. Much detailed criticism of phrases and words in "The Dry Salvages" and "Little Gidding" came from John Hayward, who was proud of having supplied the phrase "the laceration of laughter," with its echo of Swift's epitaph. Arnold Bennett was asked to help an inexperienced dramatist to write the play of which we have only the two fragments in *Sweeney Agonistes*, and Martin Browne has told how pliable Eliot was as a dramatist, and how willing to accept suggestions and criticism from his producer and from the actors in his plays.

At times, of course, he dug in his heels. He refused to cut on Pound's advice the "No, I am not Prince Hamlet" passage in "Prufrock," saying it was essential—as indeed it is, for the heroism of Hamlet in daring to formulate the "overwhelming question" contrasts his indecision with Prufrock's, who is no hero. The fact that he neither revised nor suppressed his early poems suggests that however much he had changed he respected their integrity as poems. There had been a time for them; it was now time for another way of writing. Change and continuity is the theme of his last great poem on Time the preserver and Time the destroyer. In discussing Eliot one has to stress both.

This devotion to his vocation as a poet, to poetry as an art to be learned from the study and assimilation of the work of its great practitioners, made Eliot, as Robert Lowell has recently declared, the hero of many in the next generation of poets. Others, and they were by no means only Philistines, were unattracted by a poetry so much the product of will and conscious choice and intellectual decisions. To them the poetry of Eliot seemed to display a factitious originality, to be a pseudoscholarly excogitation of a highly selective version of the European tradition, containing good lines and good passages but lacking in creative energy and imaginative sympathy, overcerebral and overliterary: a patchwork poetry made up of scraps pieced together and eked out by parody. The debate continues, and I suspect that it always will. For Eliot is a poet of a particular kind, a kind that divides opinion, rousing a strong response in some who treasure his poetry for its deliberation and as strong a distaste in others who, while owning his skill and his seriousness, feel his poetry to be fatally narrow in range and lacking in the "roll, the rise, the carol, the creation." They also, and this applies to many who admire aspects of his work, find antipathetic that strongly Puritan strain in his personality as man and poet which links him so oddly with Milton, whom he attacked, and Wordsworth, whom he virtually ignored. Like them he is a poet of "the egotistical sublime," with a powerful poetic personality, the opposite of Keats's poet, who has, as poet, "no Identity."

Eliot, by deliberate and conscious choice and effort of will, first made and then remade himself as a poet. Starting from the late Romantic tradition in England and America, he broke from it radically and made himself a European poet by a bold assimilation of very varied styles. Only one poet remained as an influence with him throughout his life: Dante, whom he read first at Harvard. In his middle life he remade himself, as a man and a poet, with great courage, discipline, and pain. He did so by going back to his original foundations—to his childhood and youth—and attempted in his last great poem to include and bring into a pattern all his experience as child, young man, American, and European, refusing nothing that had happened to him as man and artist.

He brought back into his poetry what he had earlier repudiated, his nineteenth-century heritage, and developed a new style all his own, expressive in its variety and remarkable for its accent of personal truth. This new style could accommodate the brilliant images, and the haunting phrases—for Eliot is one of the great masters of the unforgettable poetic phrase—that marked his poetry from the beginning; but it also allowed him to modulate from personal reflection to philosophic exploration of ideas and meanings, and to include in his poetry general statements.

This new style first appeared in *Ash-Wednesday*, where the poet drops his mask, forgets his cherished doctrine of impersonality and speaks to us candidly as "I":

> Because I do not hope to turn again
> Because I do not hope
> Because I do not hope to turn
> Desiring this man's gift and that man's scope
> I no longer strive to strive towards such things

Its appearance coincides with the final breakdown of his tragic first marriage and with his baptism and confirmation. These two experiences, the long-drawn-out agony of his first marriage and his acceptance of the discipline of religious commitment, are the twin subject of his later poetry and plays. They are concerned with the attempt to find "somewhere on the other side of despair" that which "forever renews the earth," with the leap in the dark, the venture of faith, the deliberate choice of hope against despair, the decision to rejoice, "having to construct something/Upon which to rejoice," or, to use his own image from *Marina,* with the struggle to "build a boat."

> Bowsprit cracked with ice and paint cracked with heat.
> I made this, I have forgotten
> And remember.
> The rigging weak and the canvas rotten
> Between one June and another September.
> Made this unknowing, half conscious, unknown, my own.
> The garboard strake leaks, the seams need caulking.

They are concerned also with the effort to learn how to love; with the effort of the will and the conscience to practice what ways of love are possible when loving has brought pain and agony and the sense of failure and guilt; and with learning how to live with the burdens on one's conscience.

All Eliot's poetry from "Portrait of a Lady," his first masterpiece, is concerned with deeply troubling, and also with precious but rare, experiences. For all the range of his observation, its width and shrewdness, the breadth of his intellectual interests and culture, the depth and variety of his friendships—he was a conspicuously loyal friend—his subject matter is confined. He recurs again and again to the same situations, situations that involve some kind of moral distress, as he does to the same images. I am not referring simply to his fondness for certain symbols that are obviously symbols—lilacs, hyacinths, the rose-garden, yew trees, the desert—but his obsessive interest in times and seasons, times of day, the quality of months, the process of the year from spring to winter, and also what Leonard Unger has recently pointed out: his recurrent use of images of stairs and doors, stairs one ascends or descends or stands on, stairs on which one hesitates or stumbles, doors to be opened or looked through: "I mount the stairs and turn the handle of the door/And feel as if I had mounted on my hands and knees."

He began as a poet of observation, attempting to escape from the personal and confessional, concentrating on the evocation of a scene or a mood, eschewing all reflection in the attempt to catch the moment as it was. He avoided the expression of general ideas, and found for himself deliberate disguises, adopting various quasi-dramatic roles: Prufrock, Gerontion, the little old man, or Tiresias, the blind bisexual consciousness behind *The Waste Land*. He ended as a great poet of memory and desire and aspiration, who had learned to speak with his own voice. I find the voice of the later Eliot very moving in prose as well as poetry. The remarkable note of authority in the early critical essays corresponds to the brilliant surface of the earlier poetry. The later criticism is tentative and relaxed, the voice of a man who is ready to confess that he has changed his mind. Its gentleness and dry self-deprecating humor have been attacked as timidity, and its qualifications mocked at. I find it refreshing to listen to a critic not so much in love with himself as to be unable to do anything but repeat the insights of his youth. "Gentleness and justice, these are the marks of his later criticism," wrote I. A. Richards, adding: "The only writer he is rough with in these later pages is himself . . . I doubt if another critic can be found so ready to amend what he had come to consider his former aberrations. There was more to this, I think, than just getting tired of long-occupied positions. These reversals and recantations strike me as springing from an ever deepening skepticism, a questioning of the very roots of critical pretensions."[8] The same skepticism, integrated into faith,[9] gives its peculiar quality of unauthoritative authority to the later verse.

Eliot was endowed with brilliant intellectual gifts, the power to work hard and develop them, and an acute sensibility. He responded deeply to certain rare and fleeting moments. He also recoiled from ugliness, shabbiness, ignobility, and vulgarity, recoiling with a violence that revealed a fascination. "You attach yourself to loathing as others do to loving," Agatha says to Harry in *The Family Reunion*, in what is surely a piece of profound self-criticism. He was also gifted with gaiety, charm, wit, and humor. But it was not for nothing he came of Puritan New England stock. He was from the beginning a poet of the conscience. He was capable of great moral suffering and developed the moral strength and integrity of purpose to live with pain and explore its roots without self-pity or indulgence in self-disgust. He entered very deeply into the still unresolved crisis of this century, a crisis of unbelief, failure of purpose, loss of hope, in which "the best lack all conviction." His earlier poetry, under its dazzling wit, conveys a sense of desolate meaninglessness, of pointless, purposeless activities, social and cultural, lives "measured out with coffee spoons" in rooms where women "come and go" indulging in cultured conversation, overlaying the basic realities of human existence, "birth, copulation, and death." His Waste Land is a land of sterile desires and panic fears and futile illusions and dreams of happiness, set in a present context of the loneliness of great cities and of the breaking of nations, the collapse of civilizations into anarchy. Through entry into himself to find the sources of his own pain, and his own sense of loss and despair, through exploration of his own past, and through submission to the religious tradition of Europe, as he had earlier as a poet submitted himself to its poetic tradition, he came to a sense of meaning in personal experience and in human history. I cannot believe that future ages—if mankind has a future on this planet, and those who accused Eliot of too gloomy a view of human history now look rather foolish—will not respect in Eliot's poetry the voice of the conscience of civilized man speaking out of an age of anxiety and despair, and that even those who reject the formulations of his faith will not respond to the accent of faith, and honor him as a man and a poet who chose not to despair.

[8] *Ibid.,* p. 28.
[9] See the essay on "The *Pensées* of Pascal," *Essays Ancient and Modern* (1936), pp. 150-151.

Bibliography

PRIMARY SOURCES

Only the major published works are listed here. For additional items, see the entries listed as secondary sources below.

Poetry and Drama

The Collected Poems, 1909-1962. London: Faber & Faber, 1963.

The Collected Plays. London: Faber & Faber, 1962.

The Complete Poems and Plays, 1909-1950. New York: Harcourt, Brace & World, 1952. Includes most of Eliot's work except *The Confidential Clerk* (Faber & Faber, 1954; Harcourt, Brace & World, 1954) and *The Elder Statesman* (Faber & Faber, 1959; Farrar, Straus and Cudahy, 1959).

T. S. Eliot, The Waste Land, A Facsimile and Transcript. Edited by Valerie Eliot. New York: Harcourt Brace Jovanovich, 1971.

Prose

The Sacred Wood. London: Methuen, 1920.

Homage to John Dryden. London: L. and V. Woolf, 1924.

Selected Essays, 1917-1932. London: Faber & Faber, 1932; New York: Harcourt, Brace, 1932. (Enlarged editions, called *Selected Essays*, were published in New York in 1950 and in London in 1951.)

The Use of Poetry and the Use of Criticism. London: Faber & Faber, 1933; Cambridge, Mass.: Harvard University Press, 1933.

After Strange Gods. London: Faber & Faber, 1934; New York: Harcourt, Brace, 1934.

Elizabethan Essays. London: Faber & Faber, 1934.

Essays Ancient and Modern. London: Faber & Faber, 1936; New York: Harcourt, Brace, 1936.

The Idea of a Christian Society. London: Faber & Faber, 1939; New York: Harcourt, Brace, 1940.

Notes towards the Definition of Culture. London: Faber & Faber, 1948; New York: Harcourt, Brace, 1949.

On Poetry and Poets. London: Faber & Faber, 1957; New York: Farrar, Straus and Cudahy, 1957.

Knowledge and Experience in the Work of F. H. Bradley. London: Faber & Faber, 1964.

To Criticize the Critic and Other Writings. New York: Farrar, Straus & Giroux, 1965.

SECONDARY SOURCES

Bibliographical Materials

Gallup, Donald C. *T. S. Eliot: A Bibliography*. 2d ed. London: Faber & Faber, 1969. (Originally published by Faber & Faber in 1947 and by Harcourt, Brace, 1953 and 1969.)

Martin, Mildred. *A Half-Century of Eliot Criticism: An Annotated Bibliography of Books and Articles in English, 1916-1965*. Lewisburg, Pa.: Bucknell University Press, 1972.

Biographies

Howarth, Herbert. *Notes on Some Figures Behind T. S. Eliot*. Boston: Houghton Mifflin, 1964.

Kirk, Russell. *Eliot and His Age*. New York: Random House, 1971.

Levy, William Turner and Victor Scherle. *Affectionately, T. S. Eliot*. Philadelphia: J. B. Lippincott, 1968.

Ludwig, Richard. "T. S. Eliot." *Sixteen Modern American Authors*. Edited by Jackson R. Bryer. New York: Norton, 1973.

Read, Herbert. *T. S. E.–A Memoir*. Middletown, Conn.: Center for Advanced Studies, Wesleyan University, 1966.

Sencourt, Robert. *T. S. Eliot, a memoir*. Edited by Donald Anderson. New York: Dodd, Mead, 1971.

Criticism

Antrim, Harry T. *T. S. Eliot's Concept of Language: A Study of its Development*. Gainesville: University of Florida Press, 1971.

Austin, Allen. *T. S. Eliot, The Literary and Social Criticism*. Bloomington, Indiana: Indiana University Press, 1971.

Bantock, Geoffrey Herman. *T. S. Eliot and Education*. New York: Random House, 1969.

Barry, Mary Martin, Sister. *An Analysis of the Prosodic Structure of Selected Poems of T. S. Eliot.* Washington: Catholic University of America Press, 1969.

Bergonzi, Bernard. *T. S. Eliot.* New York: Macmillan, 1972.

Bodelsen, Carl Adolf G. *T. S. Eliot's Four Quartets, A Commentary.* Copenhagen: University Publications Fund, Rosenkilde & Bagger, 1966.

Browne, Elliott Martin. *The Making of T. S. Eliot's Plays.* London: Cambridge University Press, 1969.

Cahill, Audrey F. *T. S. Eliot and the Human Predicament.* Pietermaritzburg, S. Africa: University of Natal Press, 1967.

Cameron, James. M. *The Night Battle, Essays.* Baltimore: Helicon Press, 1963.

Caretti, Laura. *T. S. Eliot in Italia.* Bari, Italy: Adriatica, 1968.

Cattavi, Georges. *T. S. Eliot.* London: Merlin, 1966.

Chiari, Joseph. *T. S. Eliot—Poet and Dramatist.* London: Vision Press, 1972.

Drew, Elizabeth A. *T. S. Eliot, the Design of His Poetry.* New York: Scribner's, 1954.

Frye, Northrop. *T. S. Eliot.* Edinburgh: Oliver and Boyd, 1963.

Gardner, Helen. *The Art of T. S. Eliot.* 6th ed. London: Faber & Faber, 1968.

——*T. S. Eliot and the English Poetic Tradition.* Nottingham, England: Nottingham University, 1966.

George, A. G. *T. S. Eliot: His Mind and Art.* Bombay: Asia Publishing House, 1969.

Headings, Philip R. *T. S. Eliot.* New York: Twayne, 1964.

Holder, Alan. *Three Voyagers in Search of Europe, A Study of Henry James, Ezra Pound, and T. S. Eliot.* Philadelphia: University of Pennsylvania Press, 1966.

Islak, Fayek M. *The Mystical Philosophy of T. S. Eliot.* New Haven, Conn.: College and University Press, 1970.

Jones, Genesius. *Approach to the Purpose, A Study of the Poetry of T. S. Eliot.* London: Hodder and Stoughton, 1964.

Kenner, Hugh. *The Invisible Poet: T. S. Eliot.* New York: McDowell, Obolensky, 1959.

Kojecky, Roger. *T. S. Eliot's Social Criticism.* New York: Farrar, Straus & Giroux, 1972.

Lu, Fei-pai. *T. S. Eliot, The Dialectical Structure of His Theory of Poetry.* Chicago: University of Chicago Press, 1966.

Margolis, John D. *T. S. Eliot's Intellectual Development, 1922-1939.* Chicago: University of Chicago Press, 1972.

Matthiessen, F. O. *The Achievement of T. S. Eliot*. 3rd ed. New York: Oxford University Press, 1959.

Montgomery, Marion. *T. S. Eliot, An Essay on the American Magus*. Athens: University of Georgia Press, 1970.

O'Connor, Daniel. *T. S. Eliot: Four Quartets, A Commentary*. New Delhi: Aarti Book Centre, 1969.

Olney, James. *Metaphors of Self, The Meaning of Autobiography*. Princeton, N.J.: Princeton University Press, 1972.

Patterson, Gertrude. *T. S. Eliot: Poems in the Making*. New York: Barnes and Noble, 1971.

Pearce, T. S. *T. S. Eliot*. London: Evans Brothers, 1967.

Praz, Mario. *James Joyce, Thomas Stearns Eliot, due maestri dei moderni*. Torino, Italy: ERI, 1967.

Rama Murthy, V. *T. S. Eliot: Critic*. Allahabad, India: Kitab Mahal, 1968.

Smidt, Kristian. *Poetry and Belief in the Work of T. S. Eliot*. New York: Humanities Press, 1961.

Smith, Carol H. *T. S. Eliot's Dramatic Theory and Practice, From Sweeney Agonistes to The Elder Statesman*. Princeton, N.J.: Princeton University Press, 1963.

Smith, Grover C. *T. S. Eliot's Poetry and Plays: A Study in Sources and Meaning*. Chicago, University of Chicago Press, 1961.

Spears, Monroe K. *Dionysus and the City, Modernism in Twentieth-Century Poetry*. New York: Oxford University Press, 1970.

Stead, C. K. *The New Poetic*. London: Hutchinson University Library, 1964.

Thompson, Eric. *T. S. Eliot, The Metaphysical Perspective*. Carbondale: Southern Illinois University Press, 1963.

Unger, Leonard. *T. S. Eliot, Moments and Patterns*. Minneapolis: University of Minnesota Press, 1966.

Verma, Rajendra. *Royalist in Politics: T. S. Eliot and The Political Philosophy*. London: Asia Publishing House, 1968.

Watkins, Floyd. *The Flesh and the Word; Eliot, Hemingway, Faulkner*. Nashville: Vanderbilt University Press, 1971.

Weinberg, Kerry. *T. S. Eliot and Charles Baudelaire*. The Hague: Mouton, 1969.

Wilks, A. J. *A Critical Commentary on T. S. Eliot's "The Waste Land."* London: Macmillan, 1971.

Williams, Helen. *T. S. Eliot: The Waste Land*. London: Arnold, 1968.

Williamson, George. *A Reader's Guide to T. S. Eliot*. 2d ed. London: Thames and Hudson, 1967.

Wright, George T. *The Poet in the Poem: The Personae of Eliot, Yeats, and Pound*. Berkeley: University of California, 1960.

Anthologies

Bergonzi, Bernard. *Four Quartets: A Casebook*. London: Macmillan, 1970.

Braybrooke, Neville. *T. S. Eliot: A Symposium for His Seventieth Birthday*. New York: Farrar, Straus and Cudahy, 1958.

Clark, David R. *Twentieth Century Interpretations of Murder in the Cathedral*. Englewood Cliffs, N.J.: Prentice-Hall, 1971.

Cox, C. B. and A. P. Hinchliffe. *The Waste Land: A Casebook*. London: Macmillan, 1968.

Kenner, Hugh. *T. S. Eliot, A Collection of Critical Essays*. Englewood Cliffs, N.J.: Prentice-Hall, 1962.

Knoll, Robert. *Storm over The Waste Land*. Chicago: Scott, Foresman, 1964.

Litz, A. Walton. *Eliot in His Time, Essays on the Occasion of the Fiftieth Anniversary of The Waste Land*. Princeton, N.J.: Princeton University Press, 1973.

March, Richard and Tambimuttu. *T. S. Eliot, A Symposium*. Freeport, Long Island: Books for Libraries Press, 1949, 1968.

Martin, Graham, ed. *Eliot in Perspective, A Symposium*. New York: Humanities Press, 1970.

Martin, Jay. *A Collection of Critical Essays on The Waste Land*. Englewood Cliffs, N.J.: Prentice-Hall, 1968.

Rajan, B. *T. S. Eliot, A Study of His Writings by Several Hands*. New York: Funk and Wagnalls, 1948.

Unger, Leonard. *T. S. Eliot, A Selected Critique*. New York: Rinehart, 1948.

Catalog

If you are interested in a list of fine Paperback
books, covering a wide range of subjects
and interests, send your name and address,
requesting your free catalog, to:

McGraw-Hill Paperbacks
1221 Avenue of Americas
New York, N.Y. 10020